COMMON OWNI

Composite 57

Conference welcomes the 1993 Conference decision to reaffirm Labour's commitment to clause IV(4) of the party constitution.

Conference notes with concern that the electoral strategy currently being pursued by the shadow cabinet places little emphasis on this constitutional aim.

Conference moves that the Parliamentary Labour Party adopts a firmer public line on issues of social justice.

Conference believes that to achieve a fair society, the redistribution of wealth must be a prime aim. To achieve this, the taxation system and public ownership should be used. Labour must present itself as a real and credible alternative. The party must inspire hope and enthusiasm. If we are to win the battle of hearts and minds, we have to offer people a real sense of the difference a Labour government will make to their lives.

Conference recalls that Labour won elections when it presented itself as a united team with a radical programme for national regeneration.

Conference strongly believes that to win, Labour must set out a positive and radical agenda which will unlock the great energies of the labour movement.

Conference must recognise where the core Labour support resides and be prepared to reinforce its strength.

Conference believes that Labour must be presented as a far more distinctive party and should be demonstrating this by making use of MPs and members from all shades of party opinion. Accordingly, Conference resolves to reinstate into Labour's manifesto the commitment to bring about a fundamental and irreversible shift in the balance of wealth and power in favour of working people and instructs that the popular objective of public ownership be fully incorporated into the party's policies.

Conference calls on the National Executive Committee to draw up a socialist economic, industrial and social strategy which will give effect to this priority; give credibility to our pledges to bring about high levels of employment and a better welfare state; enable minority groups (disabled, gays, ethnic minorities, etc.) to benefit to the same extent as all other working men and women; and make Labour a clear alternative to the other parties.

Moved by: Glasgow Maryhill CLP
Seconded by: South Derbyshire CLP

COMMON OWNERSHIP

Clause IV and the Labour Party

KEN COATES MEP

with chapters by
Clement Attlee
Michael Barratt Brown
John Hughes
Sidney Webb

SPOKESMAN

First published in Great Britain in 1995 by
Spokesman
Bertrand Russell House
Gamble Street
Nottingham, England
Tel. 0115 9708318
Fax. 0115 9420433

British Library Cataloguing in Publication Data available on request from
the British Library.

ISBN 0-85124-573-0
ISBN 0-85124-574-9 pbk

Printed by the Russell Press Ltd, Nottingham
(Tel. 0115 9784505)

Contents

Introduction

Many people have not quite understood the reason why passions in the Labour Party run so high in such apparently arcane matters as Clause IV.

The passions are about a thoroughly modern problem. The last time that Clause IV was in jeopardy, its opponents were men of very firm commitment to equality. (Not "arithmetic" equality, to be sure: but not Orwellian equality either.) They could, with reason, point to the sustained achievement of full employment, and the virtues of a seller's market for labour. That did set people free, and, had it endured, possibly socialism might have perished for a very long time.

But it did not endure. We now have mass misery on a scale which none of us have ever imagined. Millions of people subsist on the most miserable benefits, or in the corners of the black economy. In my Constituency, there are villages which are totally isolated from the modern economy, in which the men have been unable to work for a decade or more. Those who can find work often find wages which have been reduced below any decent level.

I have been trying very hard to support the Delors project for a European Keynes-plus effort to cut the unemployment figures by half, by creating 15 million new jobs before the end of the century. But the Council of Ministers, aided by our own Government, have withheld the authorisation for the raising of the necessary funds, so that rather than cutting unemployment by half, we are probably at present set on course for doubling it.

Clause IV would encourage not only the resolution of such modern problems as the robbery of pension funds, but also it could stimulate local enterprises and the expansion of public services, which might make a certain contribution to the resolution of our problem. Public environmental action could also contribute. But there is a serious lack of the political will to deal with this issue as the priority of all priorities.

Above all things today, the text which needs to be considered by the Labour Party, and by all other men and women of goodwill, is that elections are about the people's condition: "For what has a man profited, if he shall gain the whole world, and lose his own soul?" (Matthew 16,26).

Ken Coates
February, 1995

CHAPTER ONE

Opening a Debate

The objectives of the Labour Party are, for the third time this century, and before the beginning of the new millennium, to be the subject of a profound discussion within the whole Labour movement. These objectives have, since 1918, been defined in the famous Clause IV (4) of the Party's constitution:

> "To secure for the workers by hand or by brain the full fruits of their industry and the most equitable distribution thereof that may be possible upon the basis of the common ownership of the means of production, distribution and exchange, and the best obtainable system of popular administration and control of each industry or service."[1]

Speaking at the Labour Party Conference on the 4th October 1994, the new Labour Leader, Tony Blair, called for a debate on that section of the Party constitution which contains this commitment. "We have not changed to forget our principles", he said, "but to fulfil them. Not to lose our identity but to keep our relevance . . . Let us have the confidence once again that we can debate new ideas, new thinking, without for ever fearing the taunt of betrayal. Let us say what we mean and mean what we say."[2]

It is right to welcome this debate, which can help the Labour Party to reaffirm its commitment to socialism, and to focus its ideas on the profound changes which are needed as we move into the 21st century.

But this debate does not at all need to repudiate Labour's past. It should serve both to defend and extend principles which were right in the past because they already looked to the future.

Clause IV insists on three crucial commitments: to equality, to public and social ownership, and to democracy in society and at work. Since none of these commitments can be separated from the socialist project, this Clause in our constitution remains entirely valid. The language is slightly old-fashioned, because the text was drafted by Sidney Webb in 1917,[3] and adopted at a Labour Party Conference at the beginning of 1918. But the thinking remains as relevant as ever it was.

Webb affirmed his idea of "common ownership" as a continuation of the tradition of John Stuart Mill and "a repudiation of the individualism that characterised all the political parties of the past generation, and that still dominates the House of Commons".[4] Aggressive individualism had a new rebirth with the rise to authority and power of Mrs Thatcher, who unleashed an orgy of selfishness, which has deeply undermined social solidarity. Webb, by contrast, believed that individuals should join their forces, and he said that

> ". . . the programme of the Labour Party is, and will probably remain, less important . . . than the spririt underlying the programme, that spirit which gives any party its soul.
>
> The Labour Party stands essentially for revolt against the inequality of circumstance that degrades and brutalises and disgraces our civilisation.
>
> It abhors and repudiates the unscientific and immoral doctrine that the competitive struggle for the means of life is, in human society, either inevitable or requisite for the survival of the fittest; it declares, indeed, in full accord with science, that competition produces degradation and death, whilst it is conscious and deliberate co-operation which is productive of life and progress."[5]

It may be thought that these sentiments still unite the overwhelming majority of Labour Party members, and indeed, many other socially aware people outside the ranks of the Party. Certainly there is no sense in which the new debate can repudiate such old ideas. They are a part of our social inheritance and they have exercised a profound influence not only on the ethos of the Labour movement, but on British public life, over the decades.

There was an extended debate on Labour's principles in 1959 and 1960, when the then Leader, Hugh Gaitskell, sought to establish a revision of the Party objects "in the light of the historic achievements of the first majority Labour Government". This discussion aroused strong passions, but in the end it resulted in the adoption (in 1960) of a statement which "reaffirms, amplifies and clarifies Party objects".[6]

The statement contained 12 points, one of which insisted that greater equality and democracy "can be achieved only through an expansion of common ownership substantial enough to give the community power over the commanding heights of the economy". The Gaitskell statement was at the time frequently described as "the new testament" by contrast with the old, as represented in Sidney Webb's version. But, against the precedents, the new testament was forgotten more quickly than the old. Nonetheless, the Gaitskell points include a strong repudiation of racial discrimination, which the Labour Party would certainly agree to reaffirm today.

None of us can rewrite our history. To rescind Clause IV would not only be an absurd and pointless act of self-mutilation, but would also be completely ineffective if the Party remained in fact committed to its aspirations. Were we to haul down the flag, whilst maintaining our beliefs, this would become apparent to all as a form of hypocrisy. No-one, however, is suggesting that we should abandon those beliefs. Most people will agree with Tony Blair that in the discussion of our objectives "we must say what we mean and mean what say", and change "not to forget our principles but to fulfil them".

Any new statement which is calculated to explain and develop our historical commitments will need to reaffirm our foremost priority, of full employment. During the 1960 debate, it was generally assumed that this battle was over, because Labour had won it.[7] Very nearly full employment was established for a period of three decades. There is no clearer evidence of the inefficiency and immorality of the capitalist market than this: mass unemployment has again become a fact of life in all the "advanced" countries, whilst poverty, misery and starvation rule a large part of the underdeveloped world. Our discussion should centre on how to eliminate these unacceptable conditions.

On the three basic commitments of Clause IV, it is necessary to begin new advances.

1. Equality

Of course Labour is committed to equality of opportunity, but this is nothing like enough. Even at the height of the welfare state, there have always been large numbers of people excluded from participation in the concerns, and in the standards, of the majority. Mrs Thatcher unleashed the market, red in tooth and claw, and with it a veritable polarisation of society. Health, education, social standards, are all fiercely divided by social class.[8] The diseases of poverty have begun to reappear. In practical terms, all will agree on the need for a national minimum wage. What of the national maximum? The maxim of modern capitalism has been an old one: "To him that hath shall be given, and from him that hath not shall be taken away, even the little which he hath." Socialism will mean a profound redistribution of income and wealth, but above all of power, which is the key to real equality.

2. Public Ownership

Sidney Webb said that his draft for Clause IV deliberately left open the choice of forms of common ownership "from the co-operative store to the nationalised railway". Today, the nationalised industries have been dwarfed by the emergence of transnational enterprises, and the "commanding heights" are often run off-shore. The big multinational corporations centre their research and development in sheltered havens, often far removed from their main production facilities. Beyond doubt this means that public ownership needs to move in two directions at once: up to the transnational level, and down to the local and regional level. Surely the European Central Bank will be a public institution? And are not combines or co-operatives of public corporations necessary in such vital fields as telecommunications and transport?

With all their faults, the nationalised industries in Britain took over some of the most backward plants and enterprises, and brought them from dereliction to the very peak of performance. Nationalised coal generated the highest safety records, the most advanced scientific expertise, and the most sophisticated technology and equipment. Private capitalism will restore this industry to the Victorian age, and situate it in the deepest squalor and poverty.

While some privatised industries must be recuperated by the public sector, Harold Wilson seized on an important truth when he advised us that public enterprise should enter the growth sector of the economy, and not restrict itself to the nationalisation of losses.

Since 1918, there has been a continuing argument about the relationship between ownership and control. Labour has got the worst of this argument for a large part of the time. Nowhere can this more clearly be seen than in the domain of pension funds, which represent deferred wages, and should clearly be the property of the workforce, together with those who have retired. But normally, such funds are not under the control of any representatives of the workforce.[9] The establishment of democratic control of all such funds would today totally transform the prospects of common ownership and worker participation.

3. Democracy

It is in this field that most remains to be done. In recent years, local democracy has been undermined, both by cuts in public expenditure, and the remorseless advance of unaccountable quangos. There is a strong case for a commitment to de-centralisation, extending the idea of "subsidiarity" to establish a firm constitutional basis for local and regional government. Industrial democracy has been under violent attack, partly as a result of mass unemployment, and partly as a result of destructive legislation. The crisis in the government of the state has been deepened by corruption, and single-party monopoly. British institutions have never sunk lower in public esteem, to the point at which the political process itself has been brought into contempt.

The restoration of democracy requires a constitutional reform, not only to establish Scottish and Welsh Parliaments, but also to devolve real powers to the English regions. If the

Second Chamber were drawn from these regions, it could be given a constitutional veto, to prevent, in future, such scandals as the curtailment of local government powers by recent Westminster administrations.

The goal of empowering our citizens, and enabling them to develop their full potential, will never be realised in the centralised state of the British establishment.

Labour should reassert the vision of William Morris, that no man or woman is good enough to be another's master. No-one should exercise power over another person, without the freely given consent of that person. All such power should be accountable, and limited in duration, subject to the consent of those over whom it is exercised.

There are a multiplicity of proposals which aim to advance each of these general principles. But one thing is absolutely clear: we shall not advance our understanding of what is necessary if we cannot defend the ground we have already won.

Clause IV, of course, contains a great deal more than the famous sub-section about these vital Party objectives. Sub-sections 6 and 7 deal with international relations. Sub-section 6 is completely out of date, since it primarily refers to the Commonwealth. Surely this sub-section could be repealed, and replaced with a similar short paragraph defining our relations with fraternal parties in the European Union? Sub-section 7 is still relevant, but might usefully be extended to include a phrase giving our own definition of the New World Order, against racism and nationalism, and promoting solidarity between the peoples.[10]

Footnotes

1. The main text was adopted at the Labour Party Conference on Friday, February 26th 1918. The words "distribution and exchange" were added in 1929, as a result of amendments proposed by the Bristol Labour Party. This change was agreed without debate.
2. Speech by Tony Blair to the Labour Party Conference on Tuesday 4th October 1994.
3. An earlier draft had been prepared by Arthur Henderson. It concentrated on the need for public ownership of monopolies. This is what Henderson proposed:
   "To secure for the producers by hand or brain the full fruits of their industry by the common ownership of all monopolies and essential raw materials."
   For an account of the discussion of this draft, see Ross McKibbin: *The Evolution of the Labour Party 1910-1924*, Oxford University Press, 1974, Chapter 5.

The difference between the 1918 constitution and the earlier consitution of 1914, which it replaced, are fully set out in G.D.H. Cole: *History of the Labour Party from 1914*, Routledge and Kegan Paul, 1948, pp.56-81.

4. Sidney Webb expanded the thinking behind Clause IV in an article in *The Observer* in 1917. Later this was reprinted as a Labour Party pamphlet. This was republished in *Tribune* on Friday February 26th 1960, during the debate on the reform of the Labour Party constitution, initiated by Hugh Gaitskell at the Labour Party Conference in 1959. See Chapter Two.

5. *Ibid.*

6. This statement was republished in Philip Williams' biography: *Hugh Gaitskell*, Jonathan Cape, 1978, pp.572-3. See Chapter Five.

7. The classic statement of this view was made by C.A.R. Crosland, in *The Future of Socialism*, published by Jonathan Cape, in 1956.

8. See Andrew Glyn and David Miliband: *Paying for Inequality*, IPPR/Rivers Oram Press, 1994. This study establishes that the gap between the highest and lowest paid in the UK is now greater than it has been at any time since 1886. During the five years up to 1992, the top directors of the top 100 companies received pay increases of 133%, to reach an average salary of £535,000. During the same time, the lowest paid 10% of workers received increases totalling 38%. The study establishes that the richest 1% of the population own 129 times more marketable wealth than the least wealthy 50% of the British population. At the same time, 31% of children now live in households whose income is less than half the average income. In the last two years before Mrs Thatcher's election, only 10% of British children were in this state of poverty. On the question of the tax burden, Glyn and Miliband established that the bottom 10% of the population pays 43% of its income in tax, whilst the top 10% pays only 32%. Between 1979 and 1992 there were thirty-one billion pounds worth of tax cuts. The top 1% of income earners received 93 times as much of this as did the bottom half of the population.

9. See John Hughes: *Socialist Objectives and Development from within the Market Economy*, TURU, Oxford, 1994. See Chapter Ten.

10. This text was first endorsed by Peter Crampton MEP, Henry McCubbin, and Ian White MEP. An abbreviated version was prepared by Stan Newens MEP, which was subsequently signed by half the European Parliamentary Labour Party. The other MEPs who signed were Eryl McNally, Alex Falconer, Clive Needle, Barry Seal, Mike Elliott, Alex Smith, David Thomas, Tom Megahy, Stephen Hughes, Mike Hindley, Roger Barton, Hugh Kerr, Norman West, Richard Balfe, Alan Donnelly, Christine Oddy, David Hallam, Ken Stewart, Eddy Newman, Joe Wilson, Sue Waddington, Mike McGowan, Alf Lomas, Shaun Spiers, David Bowe, David Morris, Robert Evans and Hugh McMahon.

CHAPTER TWO

Clause IV

Sidney Webb

This article was written for The Observer, *to explain the thinking behind Sidney Webb's proposals for a new constitution for the Labour Party. It was published in 1917. The constitution was adopted the following year.*

The proposal to reorganise the Labour Party, formulated by its National Executive, and circulated to its constituent societies for their consideration, may well prove an event of far-reaching political importance. Instead of a sectional and somewhat narrow group, what is aimed at is now a national party, open to anyone of the 16,000,000 electors agreeing with the party programme.

More important, however, than any of these changes in the constitution is the change of spirit that has inspired them. The Labour Party, which has never been formally restricted to manual-working wage-earners, is now to be publicly thrown open to all workers "by hand or by brain".

Its declared object is to be, not merely the improvement of the conditions of the wage-earner, but "to secure for the producers, by hand or by brain, the full fruits of their industry and the most equitable distribution thereof that may be possible upon the basis of the common ownership of the means of production, and the best obtainable system of popular administration and control of each industry or service".*

---

*Historical Note: The words "distribution and exchange" were added to Clause IV of the Labour Party constitution in 1929. They were moved as amendments to the Constitution by the Bristol Labour Party and went through without any debate.

The only persons to be excluded (and that, of course, only by inference) are the unoccupied and unproductive recipients of rents and dividends — the so-called "idle rich" — whom it is interesting to find *The Times* editorially declaring to be of no use to the community.

The Labour Party of the future, in short, is to be a party of the producers, whether manual workers or brain workers, associated against the private owners of land and capital as such.

Its policy of "common ownership" brings it, as a similar evolution brought John Stuart Mill — to use his own words in the *Autobiography* — "decidedly under the general designation of Socialist."

But it is a Socialism which is no more specific than a definite repudiation of the individualism that characterised all the political parties of the past generation and that still dominates the House of Commons.

This declaration of the Labour Party leaves it open to choose from time to time whatever forms of common ownership from the co-operative store to the nationalised railway, and whatever forms of popular administration and control of industry, from national guilds to ministries of employment and municipal management, may, in particular cases, commend themselves.

What the Labour Party at present means by its Socialism is revealed in the remarkable pamphlet which it has published on its "After the War Programme", setting forth in a dozen detailed resolutions passed at the Manchester Party Conference exactly what it wishes done with the railways, the canals, the coal mines, the banking system, the demobilisation of the army and munition workers, the necessary rehousing of the people, the measures to be taken for preventing the occurrence of unemployment, the improvement of agriculture, the taxation to be imposed to pay for the war, the reform of our educational system, and what not.

Opinions will naturally differ as to some of these sweeping proposals, but no one of any education can safely denounce them as unpractical or despise them as ill-informed.

It is, indeed, one of the claims of the Labour Party that science is on their side; that it is their proposals, not those of the Liberals or those of the Unionists, that nowadays receive the general support of the "orthodox" economists; and that, as a matter of fact, it is essentially their proposals to which every Minister of State, when he is brought up against a difficult problem of administration, has actually to turn — and then to lose his nerve, emasculate what would have got over his difficulties, and produce an abortion which has the advantages neither of individualism nor of collectivism!

But the programme of the Labour Party is, and will probably remain, less important (except for educating the political leaders of other parties) than the spirit underlying the programme, that spirit which gives any party its soul.

The Labour Party stands essentially for revolt against the inequality of circumstance that degrades and brutalises and disgraces our civilisation.

It abhors and repudiates the unscientific and immoral doctrine that the competitive struggle for the means of life is, in human society, either inevitable or requisite for the survival of the fittest; it declares, indeed, in full accord with science, that competition produces degradation and death, whilst it is conscious and deliberate co-operation which is productive of life and progress.

It is unreservedly democratic in its conviction — here also fortified by political science — that only by the widest possible participation in power and the most generally spread consciousness of consent can any civilised community attain either its fullest life or its utmost efficiency. But it recognises that no mere rightness of aspiration or morality or purpose can in themselves accomplish their ends; and that for the achievement of results knowledge and the application of the scientific method is required, notably in the science of society, for the further study and endowment of which it presses.

And finally the Labour Party has faith in internationalism (as distinguished from the characteristically liberal cosmopolitanism). It repudiates all "Imperialism" or desire for domination over other races. It pleads for the right of each people to live its own life, and make its own specific contribution to the world in its own way, recognising, indeed, no one "superior race" but "reciprocal superiorities" among all races.

It is not without significance that the National Executive of the Labour Party has included, as a fundamental object of the party, the establishment of a Federation or League of Nations for such international legislation as may prove possible. No other political party has yet nailed this flag to its mast.

The Labour Party is, without doubt, today the party of inspiration and promise. Tomorrow it may well prove to be the party of the future, destined, perhaps, to play as large a part in the political history of the twentieth century as the Liberal Party did in that of the nineteenth.

Annex to Chapter Two

There follows the complete text of Clause IV of the Constitution of the Labour Party. Item 7 was added at the suggestion of Tony Benn, during the time of the Gaitskell leadership of the late 1950s. The text follows Webb's 1917-18 draft, as changed in 1929.

1. Clause IV

The objects of the Labour Party are set out in Clause IV of the party's constitution. It reads as follows:

National

1. To organise and maintain in parliament and in the country a political Labour Party.

2. To co-operate with the General Council of the Trades Union Congress, or other kindred organisations, in joint political or other action in harmony with the party constitution and standing orders.

3. To give effect as far as may be practicable to the principles from time to time approved by the party conference.

4. To secure for the workers by hand or by brain the full fruits of their industry and the most equitable distribution thereof that may be possible upon the basis of the common ownership of the means of production, distribution, and exchange, and the best obtainable system of popular administration and control of each industry or service.

5. Generally to promote the political, social and economic emancipation of the people, and more particularly of those who depend directly upon their own exertions by hand or by brain for the means of life.

Inter-Commonwealth

6. To co-operate with the labour and socialist organisations in the Commonwealth overseas with a view to promoting the purposes of the party, and to take common action for the promotion of a higher standard of social and economic life for the working population of the respective countries.

International

7. To co-operate with the labour and socialist organisations in other countries and to support the United Nations Organisation and its various agencies and other international organisations for the promotion of peace, the adjustment and settlement of international disputes by conciliation or judicial arbitration, the establishment and defence of human rights, and the improvement of the social and economic standards and conditions of work of the people of the world.

CHAPTER THREE

The Blair Initiative: Revising Socialism or Rejecting It?

The promise of a discussion on new objectives was not to be honoured in the way Party members originally expected. A very one-sided presentation was circulated throughout the Labour Party in January 1995.

Introducing their new statement on "Labour's Objects: Socialist Values in the Modern World", the Blair leadership team offer us a preliminary statement which tells us that "the Labour Party is a democratic socialist party". This goes on to offer a menu which could be presented by almost any Liberal:

> "It is founded on the simple belief that individuals prosper when supported by a strong and active society, and that people owe a duty to each other as well as themselves. It is from this central belief that our core values are derived: social justice, freedom, opportunity, equality, democracy and solidarity. Democratic socialism sees economic efficiency and social justice as complementary to one another, not opposites; and links together action to establish a prosperous and strong economy with action to attack poverty, increase employment, counter discrimination, curb unaccountable power, and protect the environment."

What is wrong with such a liberal prospectus? Certainly most of the objects appeal to elementary commonsense. Why is that insufficient?

If democratic socialism "sees economic efficiency and social justice as complementary to one another, not opposites", what measures does it propose to ensure that its vision begins to correspond to reality? Left alone, economic efficiency as it is conventionally understood stands in no relation whatever to social justice because it is not driven by either law or compassion, but by competition for growth and survival. Aneurin Bevan once summed it up with admirable economy:

> "What are the most worthy objects on which to spend surplus productive capacity? . . . After providing for the kind of life we have been leading as a social aggregate, there is an increment left over that we can use as we wish. What would we like to do with it?
>
> Now the first thing to notice is that in a competitive society this question is never asked. It is not a public question at all. It cannot be publicly asked with any advantage because it is not capable of a public decision which can be carried out. Therefore in this most vital sphere, the shaping of the kind of future we would like to lead, we are disfranchised at the very outset. We are unable to discuss it because the disposal of the economic surplus is not ours to command . . . The surplus is merely a figure of speech. Its reality consists of a million and one surpluses in the possession of as many individuals . . . If we reduce the question to the realm where we have brought it, that is to say, to the individual possessor of the surplus, the economist will provide us with a ready answer. He will tell us that the surplus owner will invest it in the goods for which he thinks there will be a profitable sale. The choice will lie with those able to buy the goods the owner of the surplus will proceed to produce. This means that those who have been most successful for the time being, the money owners, will in the sum of their individual decisions determine the character of the economy of the future . . . But . . . the kind of society which emerges from the sum of individual choices is not one which commends itself to the generality of men and women. It must be borne in mind that the successful were not choosing a type of society. They were only deciding what they thought could be bought and sold profitably." (*In Place of Fear*)

That is to say, social priorities, including social justice, *cannot* be assured simply by reliance on the market. This possesses no self-corrective mechanism for transferring individual surpluses "to attack poverty, increase employment, counter discrimination, curb unaccountable power, and protect the environment".

"Justice" has to be *outside* the market, and presupposes a capacity by the public authority to override it. But the market has been systematically eroding and dissolving all external pressures to regulate or control its operations for many years. In this respect it has enjoyed very considerable success.

In the past, action for correction could be taken, not by the market, but by Government. In pursuit of these social goals, Government might, by taxing profits and high incomes, transfer the revenue so garnered to good redistributive effect. But the Labour Party's present front bench insists that it proposes no structural shift in taxation other than the blocking of "loopholes".

Unfortunately, the main "loophole" which frustrates the tax inspector is the device of transfer pricing, which is systematically deployed by multinational corporations to transfer their profits from wherever they may have been earned, to the most beneficial area: from the point of view of tax advantages, amongst other things. Of course, transnational corporations also have to devote a lot of attention to speculation in the currency markets, in order to stay ahead in the game of competitive devaluation, which was so strongly boosted when the British Government fell out of the Exchange Rate Mechanism on Black Wednesday, September 16th, 1992. National tax inspectors all around the world chorus their lamentations about the insurmountable difficulties which are involved in imposing effective taxation on multinational capital. If it could be done, no doubt it would be difficult. But by what other magic does our Leader propose to transfer the profits of the growth sector of multinational capital, to the socially valid purpose of creating jobs, for instance?

We have lived through a decade and a half in which a wide variety of constraints on the free operation of markets have been removed. Abysmally low minimum wages, established by the Wages Councils, and policed by a diminishing band of over-stretched and ineffective inspectors, have now gone.

The resulting free-for-all means ever lower wages among the undefended poor. Competition invariably generates inequalities, but these are now less regulated than ever they were. Always, someone has lost. Now, the loss is comprehensive, obliterating.

But someone wins. The winners acquire monopoly powers over whole products and industries, and dominate all the people in them.

Before he was elected in 1964, Harold Wilson told us:

> "At every level of our national life, talent and ability are wasted; our children do not get equal opportunities or our citizens equal chances to develop their qualities and energies. In an age of great potential plenty, we are still in this country cursed by indefensible pockets of shameful poverty and injustice which twelve years of so-called affluence have not removed."

Today, the poverty no longer lives in pockets, but blankets large sections of a society which subsists in profound social crisis. To tell us that growth on its own will facilitate action for improvement is plainly not true. Perhaps growth *could* enable action to be taken, but the mechanics of such action, here, are all-important. Normally, growth will aggravate the problem. There is no such thing as "trickle down" in the field of wealth. Wealth is energetically hoovered up. What trickles down is misery, poverty, rejection and destitution.

Today most Liberals deny this, but this was not always the case. Precisely at the time when Clause IV was written, to separate the Labour Party from the paternal influence of the Liberals, there were Liberals who were able to see these truths quite plainly. Today, all these intellectual processes have gone into reverse. The most brutal forms of liberalism were espoused by Mrs Thatcher, and imposed with manic zeal. Her single-minded devotion has pulled behind her, first, middle-liberal opinion, and now, a significant part of the Labour leadership, whose hunger for office is commendably strong: but unfortunately outweighs any allegiance to its abandoned constituencies.

The new leadership statement has achieved on paper something that generations of supporters of Clause IV have never dreamt of. It has abolished capitalism. Nowhere can this dread concept be found in the new text. The text is so full of reach-me-down values that it might have been composed by Patience Strong, but for the unfortunate fact that it does not rhyme. "The process of constitutional revision", say the authors, "is intended to set out our identity as a Party in our own terms for our own age". But has capitalism really disappeared in this age of comforting and empty froth? It is true that capital has become more fluid, more mobile. At the touch of a button, millions can travel along the wires, or along the optical fibres, to disappear here and materialise in another place. Along the wires, routine tasks are transferred to low-paid Indian women, who programme the bookings for European airlines, and flash the resultant effort back in seconds. Then the prosperous stockholders can board their planes. Reality has not disappeared, but it has been beautifully concealed. Has Tony Blair got access to some of these computer buttons? Will the wires transmit his commands? And will they deliver social justice on all the screens that matter?

Alas, no. The present Labour leadership resembles nothing more than the inhabitants of those South Sea Islands which initiated the cargo cults. Observing that the missionaries who came among them lived very happy lives, the indigenous peoples made a close study of the causes of this happiness. They perceived that the missionaries wanted for nothing, and that the secret of their prosperity lay in the cargos which were ferried to them in small aeroplanes, at regular intervals. In the cargo, there was nourishment and uplift. Commentaries on scripture and crates of gin brought consolation to the foreign teachers.

Having scientific minds, the natives were quick to agree that the benefits of cargos might with profit be more widely shared among the excluded. They gathered their forces, and cleared space in the forests, where the planes could land. They lit beacons, to guide them in. And they waited. But no cargos came.

The long suffering people of Britain do not have so long to wait. No cargos are coming. Unless remedial action is taken to redistribute wealth, the poor will decline into even deeper misery. And unless a strong public force generates local enterprise, stimulates co-operation, and encourages common effort, capitalism will assiduously ensure the continuation of present trends. More polarisation, richer rich, poorer poor. These processes will continue with a Queen or without one, with hereditary Peers, or without them, and throughout whatever cosmetic changes might be made to keep hidden the realities of economic power. Is that the modern age, or isn't it?

*   *   *

The history presented in the draft document is, to say the least of it, eccentric. It correctly informs us that the first draft of Clause IV appeared in October 1917, the very month of the Bolshevik Revolution. But it goes on to tell us that central planning "had after all helped Britain to win the war". Not in October 1917 it hadn't. Neither in 1917 had the Russian Soviets established public ownership and central planning. Their first task, under a variety of forms of workers' control, was to re-establish any kind of production, with or without the help of experienced managers. In 1917 and early 1918, the current of thought that constituted a perceived threat to the Labour leadership was syndicalist, and it seemed threatening because it advocated workers' control in British factories and industries, not in those of Russia or elsewhere.

The preliminary draft for the Clause had been written by Arthur Henderson. It spoke about taking into public ownership "the monopolies". This was a long-standing commitment of Henderson's, and it was based, not on socialist doctrine, but on impeccable Victorian liberal teaching. In the philosophical writings of T.H. Green, it had been pointed out that the Hegelian justification of property as "the first reality of freedom" could no longer be invoked if property was monopolised. This is an old argument, which goes back a long way in political theory. Certainly Marx had identified the same problem that Green treated decades later. Locke had insisted, by contrast, that property was justified where men had "mixed their labour" with the gifts of nature. But this, too, hit a problem with monopoly. What could happen when all the land was occupied, and none was left vacant to be mixed with the labour of any newcomer? This was the great fascination of America, as a seemingly inexhaustible source of virgin land, in which work would generate property, and thus in Hegelian terms, freedom. But monopoly closed out newcomers, bolted the door against them. From guaranteeing freedom, such property had become inimical to it. Thus, Henderson's formula was a direct echo of more than one important strand of liberal thinking. But Webb's amended version of Clause IV cut that link.

Webb was drawing on the experience of trade unionism during the First World War, and the growth of collectivist responses.

For many workers, the years of the war marked their first experience of something approaching humane working conditions. Employers became more than willing to strike reasonable bargains with their workpeople, because many of them were now remunerated on a "cost-plus" system which guaranteed all munitions manufacturers a fixed rate of profit over and above the costs they incurred in production. Higher wages were simply higher costs, and offered no detriment to the "plus" which would be allocated to profits.

Of course the founding fathers lived always in an ambivalent relationship to Liberalism. They were deeply engaged in the commitment to individual freedom, and to the need to create scope for all to become whatever each had it in himself or herself to be. But personal advance, for most, already depended on collective betterment.

Why did Webb's wording prevail? It was precisely attuned to the trade union experience of collective advance in this kind of planned war economy, and it was finely calculated to separate trade union voters from any residual allegiance they might feel to the Liberals as a Party. Since the working class electorate was considerably enlarged in 1918, this was a crucial strategic move.

If Clause IV served to demarcate Labour from the Liberal Party in 1918, what would its removal signify in 1994? Evidently it would mean realignment, in which Liberals of either the Liberal or Conservative Parties might feel free to participate.* How participate? By voting? By supporting? By joining in a common Party? By forming a common Government? And what might the programme of such a Government be? Who would represent the unemployed, the excluded, the poor, in such an enterprise? What mechanisms would exist to aid these groups of people? And who could represent the other employees? How many of them should be nudged downwards below the poverty barrier?

Capitalism may have become invisible behind its apparatus of wires and high-tech communication. It may no longer have its national roots. It has certainly disappeared from the programme of "New Labour", which never comes near to mentioning it. But until it is displaced from its authority over our economic life, it will still call all the tunes.

The historical section of the leadership statement tells us that Clause IV was agreed because "there was genuine revulsion at the sheer anarchy and exploitation associated with the free market of Victorian capitalism". And the anarchy of modern global capitalism? The destruction of large parts of the world economy, mass starvation and civil war in former colonies across Africa, and here at home seven and a half million *long-term* unemployed in the territories of the European Community alone: is there no anarchy and exploitation there? Large tracts of Britain are crumbling into physical and moral ruins. Do we need to do sums to explain this?

Nobody, but nobody, in the Labour movement, will seek to hamper any Labour leadership, if it will tell us how it will restore hope to the forgotten people of Britain, and join forces with others to help the destitute in Africa and elsewhere. A programme for this kind of action could conceivably be an "adequate expression of what the Labour Party stands for". But such an expression will not only mention the word capitalism. It will try to analyse what has happened to capital, and seek to find appropriate ways to curtail the immense concentrations of power which it has secreted.

---

*All this has been justified in the name of Antonio Gramsci as a recipe for the creation of what is unappealingly described as a "hegemonic bloc". Poor Gramsci is revolving in his grave. It is strange to see this most principled and democratic of all Western communists pressed into service by the most unprincipled and manipulative of all opportunists.

*   *   *

This task will not yield to the efforts of one national movement alone. To match and pace global capital, international Labour co-operation becomes essential. That is why it is relevant for the Leader's draft to devote several pages to reporting the opinions of other Socialist Parties, and considering their own statements of aims and values. Thus, it reports the German Social Democrats as insisting:

> "We want fundamental economic decisions, particularly those determining what will increase and what will decrease, to be taken democratically".

Where are such decisions taken at the moment? It is surely no secret that they are normally taken in board rooms, in pursuit of this, that or the other market objective. Surely it might be a good idea to take such decisions democratically: but how?

The German system of co-determination is radically different from the system of industrial management in Britain, and opens certain democratic prospects which do not exist in our country. Even so, not many worker directors will admit today to possessing the necessary powers to fulfil this programme. Its fulfilment would require major change.

The Swedish programme is also cited. It wishes to place

> "the right of determination of production and distribution . . . in the hands of the entire nation."

This smells uncomfortably close to common ownership, which perhaps explains why, in the words of the leadership statement, the Swedish Party is "Europe's most successful".

In fact, the Swedish Party has suffered serious reverses since the early 1980s. The death of Olof Palme inflicted a terrible blow on the Swedish left, which also had to cope with a ferocious economic squeeze, in very difficult circumstances. The SAP entered a period of "liberalism" in the middle '80s, deregulating financial markets and phasing out all exchange controls. Tax reforms annulled the more progressive features of redistributive policy, extended Value Added Tax, and eliminated graduated tax brackets for most wage earners. It is true that these years also saw increases in Capital Gains Tax.

But it cannot be said that these policies were any more popular in Sweden than they have been in other countries. Undoubtedly they contributed to the loss of office in 1991. Fortunately for the Swedes, the Bildt regime did not prove to be so durable as that of Mrs Thatcher.

Of course, the authors of the leadership statement would be right if they were referring to the century long trajectory of the Swedish Labour movement. This came to a head with the initiation of the Meidner Report of 1976. The Report proposed that companies employing more than fifty or one hundred workers should be compelled by law to issue new shares, up to a value of twenty per cent of their annual profits, to their own wage earners, taken as a collective.

Since it was envisaged that this policy should continue year on year, the higher the profits of a given firm, the more quickly its ownership would have been transferred to the workforce.

This sounds like common ownership does it not?

Certainly Swedish employers were not fond of these proposals and worked might and main to get them diluted. But it was genuinely difficult to maintain this bold policy in the face of intense international competition, when Swedish multinationals could invest outwards, and deploy all the arts of transfer pricing to punish Governments of which they disapproved.

However, a Meidner plan for major European corporations might be a very interesting prospect.

It is when we get to the excerpt from the French statement that we reach perhaps the most revealing territory. This is quoted as follows:

> "The *Parti Socialiste* aims at promoting through democratic means a society that reflects fundamental aspirations of humans as defined through centuries of struggle for progress and expressed today by all peoples: freedom, equality and dignity for both men and women, welfare responsibility and solidarity . . . The *Parti Socialiste* is therefore in favour of a society based on a mixed economy which — without ignoring the market's rules — provides

the public powers and social actors with the means to realise aims which conform with the general interest. It aspires to new forms of economic and social organisation, in order to give workers real citizenship within the firm."

It will be observed that before the statement says that the *Parti Socialiste* is in favour of a society based on a mixed economy, there are three dots. It is always useful to see what such dots conceal. In fact in this case three paragraphs have been deleted, one per dot. This is what they say:

"A party of unity where reform is used to fulfil revolutionary hopes. It is part and parcel of the historical development of democratic socialism.

Whilst sciences and techniques offer new opportunities for freedom and creativity, but can also destroy and pervert all forms of life, the *Parti Socialiste* is acting so that these will be beneficial to both men and women.

The *Parti Socialiste* is a party of social transformation. The failure of bureaucratic societies has not prevented the Party noting that capitalism develops inequalities, accentuates worldwide imbalances, exploits the riches of the Third World and maintains unemployment and exclusion in many countries."

Three interesting dots! Each one obliterates an unpleasant truth. Modernising dots, indeed!

The leadership statement also fails to quote the statement which says that the French Socialist Party is

"anchored in the world of work. Persistent and profound changes in contemporary societies have not eliminated confrontation between classes and social groups".

There were other statements that the leadership might have found interesting. The Belgian Socialist Party aims

"to organise — in the field of the class struggle — all socialist forces from Wallonia and Brussels without distinction."

The Italian PDS has chosen what sounds like a resonant liberal statement, which aims at an ideal society "in which 'the free development of each person is the condition for the free development of all'."

The thought has been better translated, but it was not suitable for use in the British leadership statement, because it is a direct quotation from the *Communist Manifesto*.

The leadership statement summarises this, its rather partial investigation, by saying:

"Key themes run through these statements: a desire for a society which seeks for its people liberty, equality, democracy, social justice; a dedication to replace class divisions with communities in which people support and cooperate with one another; a commitment to international peace; and a determination to build a society which uses the economy to achieve these ends."

And all of this sounds quite nice. But how can politicians "use" the economy, when they have next to no control over it? Global capitalism is calling the tune, and the politicians are dancing to it. Indeed, some Labour politicians are dancing quite elegantly, but we need our own tune.

We could, in association with socialists in a number of other nations, consolidate our forces to use what economic instruments we have, or could invent, to influence the behaviour of these global corporations. One of the influences might very well be the joining together of transnational public enterprises, or the creation of co-operative combines. But "determination" to build a new society will not last long in a political frame which lacks any of the effective means for realising such aspirations.

CHAPTER FOUR

Whatever Happened to Capitalism?

Michael Barratt Brown

The Core Values

The NEC statement on *Labour's Objects: Socialist Values in the Modern World* proclaims the core values of a Democratic Socialist Party as "social justice, freedom, opportunity, equality, democracy and solidarity."

The statement recognises that some of these values may sometimes be in conflict: opportunity for some may deny freedom to others; unregulated freedom can create inequality; democracy, if it is no more than the rule of the majority, may deny social justice to the minority; freedom today may destroy opportunities tomorrow.

The statement therefore speaks of countering discrimination, of curbing unaccountable power, of markets requiring regulation, of monopoly on service delivery justifying public ownership, of collective action for the common good, of reorganising society better to preserve the future against environmental degradation.

Nonetheless, at the heart of the statement comes a clear commitment to what is called the "insight" at what is the basis of socialism:

> "We are all social beings, people connected to other people, rather than isolated individuals independent of each other. Human life is a network of social relations — relations at their best marked by trust, cooperation, and partnership — rather than competition, greed and deception."

This is followed by a similarly clear commitment to democracy for a *democratic* socialist party:

> "One of the first and most basic demands of socialists was for the extension of democracy, first through universal suffrage, then more widely in the institutions of society and economy. Democracy means rule by the people so that every institution in our society and economy is accountable to those who (*sic*) it serves."

The Competitive Market Economy

When it comes to translating these values into practical aims the statement proposes:

> "We believe in an economy that works in the public interest. *A competitive market economy* (emphasis added) with a strong industrial and wealth generating base is in the public interest. So are well run public services. To achieve both, we need not just a thriving private sector but an enterprising public sector where there will of course be a role for public ownership for reasons of efficiency as well as justice. For example, essential public services should treat all citizens equally on the basis of their common humanity and not unequally on the basis of their purchasing power."

In support of these last propositions, the statement claims that

> "Socialists all over the world work to advance the cause of socialism within the *mixed economy* (emphasis added). Labour is no different. The mixed economy depends on the rules that govern markets as well as the size of the public sector . . ."

In the examples that are given of democratic socialist parties' constitutions — in Germany, Sweden, France — and in the Socialist International's Declaration of Principles, only in the French is there any reference to the mixed economy, and this has been most sharply contested at the latest congress of the *Parti Socialiste*. The NEC did not choose to include quotations from the constitutions of the Belgian and other European socialist parties which include outright denunciations of capitalist exploitation in the market, as does the Swedish constitution in a section that is also not quoted.

Clause IV of the Labour Party's constitution, agreed in 1918, with its commitment to "common ownership" and the "best obtainable system of popular administration" in order to "secure for the workers by hand or by brain the full fruits of their industry and the most equitable distribution thereof" is said by Mr Blair to need restating "in its proper context — as part of a mixed economy".

This historic commitment to common ownership in 1918 is said by the NEC to have been "the product of revulsion at the failures of 19th Century free market capitalism — pauperism, unemployment, mass poverty and exploitation . . . The prevailing view was that because unregulated markets had failed, they had to be replaced."

There need be no doubt about the causes of our forebears' revulsion, but the question is whether the causes in free market capitalism of the failures which so revolted them have been eradicated, or whether the failures persist and unregulated markets have still to be replaced.

Can anyone really believe that "pauperism, unemployment, mass poverty and exploitation" have been eradicated even in our own country, one of the most developed of the market economies, let alone in the so-called "developing countries" where five sixths of the world's peoples live?

In the UK alone, what of the current 10% of people seeking work who are unemployed, one million for over a year?

What of the one fifth of the population, including one third of the children, who live in poverty, according to Department of Social Security figures?

What of the half million who are homeless?

What of the 13 millions whose pay is below half the national average?

What of the 21 million who cannot afford a holiday or celebration?

What of the 3 million part-time women employees who have no protection from national insurance?

The Market Today
The NEC seeks to recommend to us their belief in the

competitive market economy today. How is this different from the *free market capitalism* of 1918? Is the market different? Is it no longer free but regulated or controlled? Is it now made accountable to the people? Is it competitive though not free? Is it no longer capitalist? Are the results of its workings any different? What is *the* market, anyway?

'The market' has a nice, old-fashioned ring to it; shopping on Saturday morning among the stalls in a market place, where those who seek to sell their wares have to respond to the demands of the buyers, charge a fair price or fail to clear the stock they brought. Most markets are not anything like that. *The* market comprises in effect many markets: labour markets, housing markets, commodity markets, money markets, the Stock Exchange and foreign exchanges, as well as the supermarkets and the corner shop and market stall.

Let us relate Labour's values to the actualities of the market today. At its most fundamental, does the market deal with "isolated individuals independent of each other" or does it encourage "social relations — trust, cooperation and partnership — rather than competition, greed and deception"? This, according to the NEC is, after all, the basic test of socialist values.

What are we to say, then, of Barlow-Clowes, of the BCCI, of Polly Peck, of the Maxwell Pension Funds, of insider dealing, such as Lord Archer was accused of, of all the corruption surrounding overseas contracts, of the profits made out of privatisation of state industries, and how should we explain the fact that nine tenths of all activity on the money markets and commodity markets is purely speculative?

Is any market, except the local stall-holders' market, truly competitive and truly free-for-all?

What are we to say of the monopoly power of capital, in the light of the facts

—that two or three large companies control 80% to 90% of the trade in nearly all the internationally traded commodities — food, agricultural, mineral?

—that three or four supermarket chains control two thirds of the retail business in the UK?

—that around 100 companies account for nearly 90% of all the capital issued on the UK Stock Exchange?

—that one half of all the land in Britain is owned by just one per cent of the adult population?

—that 6 per cent of the adult population own nearly 90% of the land and of company shares and 45% of the housing stock?

—that hours of work have increased on average in the last decade, one quarter of male manual workers doing more than 48 hours a week?

—that pre-tax incomes of company directors rose twice as fast in the UK between 1983 and 1992 as did average employees' earnings?

—that the pension funds of workers are used by large companies with no accountability to the fund holders?

What equality is there in the labour market for the 94% in the UK who do not own land or company shares?

What equality is there in the housing market for the 3 million households in the UK who cannot afford to buy their own homes or find public housing and must pay rent to a private landlord in housing that, in over a million cases, is regarded officially as 'unsatisfactory'?

What equality in the commodity markets is there for the millions of individual small-scale producers in the developing countries who face a single buyer for their produce?

What equality is there in shopping markets for the one fifth of all households in the UK which had only 7% of total incomes in 1989 to spend (down from 10% in 1979) compared with the top fifth which had 41% (up from 35%)?

What solidarity and what exercise of collective power can there be if the link between the Labour Party and the Trade Unions is broken and punitive laws against collective action by workers are not repealed?

When membership of trade unions in the UK has been reduced from 50% to 35% of all workers, what other protection can workers have against exploitation and worsening conditions leading to demonstrably poorer standards of health?

What measures are proposed by the NEC to ensure protection of workers against arbitrary dismissals, redundancies, asset stripping, and other such devices, since there is no mention in the statement of any form of worker representation or participation in the management of capital, despite the commitment to solidarity, opportunity and freedom?

It is not even as if private capital had a proven record of greater efficiency in return to capital or use of resources than public enterprise. Recent studies of privatisation have shown that in electricity, air transport and water supply public enterprise was superior.

Government Power to Regulate the Market

The NEC statement claims that regulation of the market can take the place of public ownership. When capital was mainly limited to operations within a single nation state, national governments could do much to regulate and even control the workings of the market.

But capital is now more than ever inter-national, operating on a global scale. National regulation is of little effect, because of the measures transnational companies can take, by transfer pricing and other internal arrangements, to avoid national taxation and national controls.

What power do governments have today to prevent the movement of funds by transfer pricing, the concealment of profits and final prices, the playing off of one government against another, which are all common practice in the accumulation of international capital?

It has been estimated that the whole accumulation of Africa's debts to foreign capital could have been prevented if African mineral producers had been paid the full market value of their product during the 1980s.

How was a British government, committed to private capital, to prevent the outflow in the decade of the 1980s of foreign direct investment from UK based companies of some £10 billions a year and portfolio investment by British capital owners of the same sum, when investment in British manufacturing industry was held down at £10 billions a year without growth?

How does the NEC expect to get the investment which the country needs in our basic industries, without a dominant element of public sector involvement? What international regulation is the NEC seeking to take the place of whatever national regulation existed previously over such concentration in the market?

Any proposals for common ownership have now to be examined on an international as well as a local basis, not just as forms of nationalisation. But what examination has been made by the NEC of intergovernmental management of telecommunications, air and rail transport, electricity and water supply, oil and natural gas?

The NEC statement makes much of the close association of Labour with socialist parties in Europe, but what proposals does the NEC have for common action to create jobs, to control capital movements, to manage public services, to make the pension funds of international companies accountable to the pensioners?

The NEC statement talks of protection of the environment and of sustainable development as important issues not included in the original Clause IV. But what measures does the NEC propose to curb the unaccountable power of giant private capitalist companies to pollute the atmosphere, destroy the natural environment, pollute the rivers and seas?

If the competitive market economy is in the public interest, how are we to prevent giant transnational capitalist companies like Union Carbide from killing thousands of Indian people, as at Bhopal, by their placing of profit before safety?

How are we to stop the transnational capitalist logging companies from ripping up the forests of the Amazon, of Ghana, of Malaysia, of Indonesia, of Papua New Guinea, of British Colombia for a short sighted profit?

And who but the giant capitalist companies are establishing cattle ranches in the burnt out Amazon lands for a short-term profit, before the land is rendered unusable?

What are we to do about the giant dam building private companies that are pushing the World Bank and those governments they can influence to finance dams in India, Malaysia, Brazil and now China, which are known by the experts to be future ecological disasters as well as immediately uprooting millions of people from their homes?

What has the NEC to say about the World Bank's structural adjustment programmes, which in the name of the competitive market economy and to collect debts due to owners of capital in Europe and North America have driven many African countries into chaos and civil war?

The NEC statement speaks of the Labour Party's commitment to international peace, but what measures does the NEC propose to reduce the sale of arms by private capitalist companies in the UK and other countries in the competitive market economy all over the world to governments which are threatened by the protests of their oppressed peoples?

How is the arms trade which has flourished as never before since the Gulf War, amounting today to nearly one fifth of all exports from the North to the South, to be brought under regulation within a competitive market economy, when it is the most profitable of all export business?

The Vision of Common Wealth

At the end of this catalogue of questions, there can be no escaping the fact that it is impossible to reconcile Labour's values with the private ownership of property — land and capital — apart from a private house and garden, a modicum of savings and a small business.

There can be no true freedom or equality or opportunity or solidarity, so long as private capital continues to be the basis of the economic system. For, private capital means that one man, or occasionally a woman, becomes another's master, deciding how they shall work, at what standard they shall live, whether they shall work at all. It means that private profit must always be put before public service.

Because attempts were made to build socialism without democracy, and these have failed, this should encourage us rather than discourage us in maintaining our search for a democratic socialist future.

Whatever compromises have to be made on the way, however much we may accept a mixed economy as an intermediate step, the goal of common wealth must remain the vision of all who call themselves democratic socialists.

By all means let us spell out our immediate aims as democratic socialists, and our special concerns for today, but all our values amount to nothing if we do not state clearly that the private ownership of capital has in the end to give way to forms of common ownership as the basis of our society. Only then shall we be able to ensure that our social relations are "marked by trust, cooperation and partnership — rather than competition, greed and deception", the ensuring of which, as the NEC correctly insists, is the hallmark of socialism.

The alternative is indeed "competition, greed and deception". It may perhaps be possible to win the necessary 40% of the votes of the adult population for policies which leave them supposedly contented with what the "competition, greed and deception" of recent governments have provided them. But, that has been at the expense of the 60% — the unemployed, pensioners, students and all the low paid, including ethnic minorities and women workers.

It is a socialist alternative that is being sought by those who have suffered most from the "competition, greed and deception" of the last decades and their interests can be joined with those of a large proportion of the supposedly contented 40% who either truly wish for a more equal society or fear the results of growing inequalities.

CHAPTER FIVE

The Debate During 1959-60

Considering matters in 1995, towards the end of a long, and alas, hitherto pointless, effort to make the Labour Party more "electable", people of a certain age become eerily aware of having heard it all before. It has taken Tony Blair's speech to the Labour Party Conference to drive us back to the archives to look at the musty pages of ancient recrimination, yellowed since 1960, and to realise that almost every word of it has now been on replay. Of course, the tone of those old arguments has not improved with age, but modern technology allows people to turn up the volume when the sense is low. In one respect the older men have the advantage: they normally spoke in sentences, since they lived before the age of sound bites, and prepacked television gibberish.

It usually happens. Then and now, politicians paid a tremendous amount of attention to the polls. Pollsters are normally ready with conventional opinions on a very wide range of matters. There is a developed art of opinion management, which can calculate the precise shape of question needed to elicit the desired answer. If there is some reason why politicians should be advised to make use of polls, there is even stronger reason to warn that it is more common for polls to make use of politicians. Clearly this has been happening continuously since Labour's defeat in the Election of 1979. But it also happened systematically in the aftermath of the earlier Labour defeat in 1951.

We are far enough away from the events of that earlier time to be able to see that the advice of pollsters was never very valuable, and sometimes positively harmful.

The war against public ownership began as soon as Mr Churchill strode back into Downing Street. There had been a very strident campaign against the nationalisation of the sugar industry, led by Tate and Lyle, the manufacturers. The press maintained a constant critical watch on the performance of the industries which had already been nationalised, and made sure that no sins of omission or commission were overlooked. Every bureaucratic excess was reported, and some were discussed at length, and repetitiously.

All this propaganda culminated in 1959, when a very large survey was commissioned by Colin Hurry Associates to demonstrate in every possible way that public ownership was unpopular, damaging, and lethal to the hopes of the Labour Party.[1] This survey was publicised with enthusiasm, and became a part of the political mythology of the times. It is not altogether surprising that it soon found echoes in the Labour Party leadership. They in turn found other pollsters who were willing to provide a great deal of "evidence" to the effect that various Labour policies were unappreciated, unpersuasive, even downright unpopular. *Socialist Commentary*,[2] the journal of a part of the right-wing establishment, which enjoyed a degree of patronage from the American Central Intelligence Agency,[3] commissioned Mark Abrams to survey public opinion, in order to discover the roots of Labour's failure.[4]

Abrams confronted 724 people with a series of sixteen statements, and asked which best expressed the spirit of the Labour Party. The five which were selected as being "outstandingly true" were these:

. . . "Stands mainly for the working class."
. . . "Is out to help the underdog."
. . . "Would extend the welfare services."
. . . "Is out to raise the standard of living of ordinary people."
. . . "Would try to abolish class differences."

Each of these statements, Abrams concluded, sees the Labour Party "essentially as a class party". There were many reasons, he concluded, "for believing that this image . . . is one unlikely to lead to a more successful future".[5] A more successful future, it seemed, might attend a party which stood mainly for the middle order of people, called the underdog strictly to heel, would curtail welfare, depress the standards of the ordinary people, and seek to maintain and reinforce class divisions. Strangely, in 1960, few dared draw such conclusions. But in 1994, they are widely embraced and loudly proclaimed. The only thing that remains persistently elusive is . . . the more successful future.

Even more of a millstone than underdoggery was public ownership. "There are few who rate (the coal industry and the railways) as successes and many more who see them as failures under public ownership." Of course, there were some who continued to favour public ownership. Eleven per cent of the sample actually wanted more of it. But there was "very little support for any extension of public ownership".

The Abrams survey sought to mobilise convenient support for those in *Socialist Commentary* who were anxious to change the name and spirit of the Labour Party. The survey had been offered to the Labour Party National Executive, before the 1959 election: but it had been rejected because it was considered too expensive.[6] However, at the beginning of 1960, *Socialist Commentary* picked up the tab. But these psephological enquiries, whilst they confirmed that young people were readier than their elders to recognise the then leader of the Labour Party, Hugh Gaitskell, as "in touch with ordinary people, practical and down to earth, straightforward and frank, and humane and kindly", also confirmed that a third of them could not think of anything specific in his Party's programme, "or else said bluntly that they did not know what was in Labour's programme".

As has often happened since, the light of hindsight shows that expensive research of this kind gives no special insights, and leads to no new understandings. Within a short time many of these young people had totally forgotten the new Labour leader, kindly or not.

The answer to the question, "must Labour lose?", was "probably yes". As Rita Hinden concluded, "Its class appeal is being undermined because the working class itself, . . . is emerging from its earlier unhappy plight". The ethos of solidarity, she thought, "is beginning to crumble". More: "promises to conquer economic distress and crises by planning based on public ownership mean little, now that the terrible economic depressions of the past appear to have been left behind".

Thoughts like this were often voiced in the months after the General Election of 1959. Hugh Gaitskell encouraged them when he convened an informal meeting at his house in Frognall Gardens, on Sunday 22nd October. The Leader's friends were mustered to devise a plan of action to transform the Labour Party in order to make it "electable".[7] (After Hugh Gaitskell died, Harold Wilson was chosen to lead the Labour Party. He succeeded in doing it without the advice of any of these strategists, contrary to every presentiment of doom. "Electable" or not, he got it elected. It is true that he did not subsequently maintain the radical promise of his campaigning days. But this shortcoming was shared in full measure with all those who had theoretically proved that the victory he won was quite impossible.)

In the depths of the 1959 defeat, general gloom prevailed. Through the murk could be heard the voices of the newspaper pundits and academics, intoning funereal dirges. Labour was now condemned to the role of opposition in permanence. Three elections had been lost, one after another. Votes had declined, by a million and a half in 1955, and by a further 200,000 in 1959. Labour supporters had begun to learn to stay at home.

Paul Johnson, at that time a scion of the left, opened the public hostilities in the *Evening Standard*. He reported that Frognall Gardens were contemplating an alliance with the Liberal Party, a possible change in the name of the Labour Party, and the total abandonment of public ownership. A new world had arrived, and the election results had proclaimed the need for these changes, to all reasonable people. Socialist fundamentalists might object, but they "were negligible".

The next contender was Douglas Jay, MP, and he chose *Forward*, a journal at that time close to Labour Party officialdom, in which to scrawl his version of the writing on the wall. A new name for the Labour Party was necessary. Further nationalisation was not required, and the proposal to reintroduce public ownership of the steel industry must be dropped. The influence of the Parliamentary Labour Party must be enhanced in a more truly federal structure, but the trade unions and the Party Conference should be reined in. The working class affinities of the Party were holding it back, and it was inappropriate to fight "under a label of a class that no longer exists".

This valediction was a little premature.

Labour Party members did not particularly wish to describe themselves as "radicals", and it was not so easy for them to come home from factories or offices, mines or schools, and follow the reasoning of Mr Jay about the disappearing working class. Constituencies began to express concern, mounting to distinct unease. But the Constituencies had in any case never elected Hugh Gaitskell to the leadership, leave alone chosen his cronies.

In those days, the Leader was chosen by the closed circle of members of the Parliamentary Party. True, Gaitskell himself had won a position on the National Executive Committee of the Party, when he stood as Treasurer. But this post depended on the block votes of the trade unions which significantly outweighed those of individual members organised in Constituencies.

Paradoxically, the same trade unions which had hitherto regarded him as a moderate man, a safe pair of hands, were shocked by Gaitskell's outbreak of radical iconoclasm. This was formally registered in a speech to the Labour Party Conference in Blackpool, in November, an uncanny pre-echo of another Blackpool oration of 1994.

"I do think that we should clear our minds on these fundamental issues and then try to express in the most simple and comprehensive fashion what we stand for in the world today.

The only official document which embodies such an attempt is the Party Constitution written over 40 years ago [1918]. It seems to me that this needs to be brought up to date. For instance, can we really be satisfied today with a statement of fundamentals which makes no mention at all of colonial freedom, race relations, disarmament, full employment or planning? The only specific reference to our objectives at home is the well-known phrase:

'To secure for the workers by hand or by brain the full fruits of their industry and the most equitable distribution thereof that may be possible, upon the basis of the common ownership of the means of production, distribution, and exchange . . .'

I hope, then, that the Executive will during the next few months try to work out and state the fundamental principles of British Democratic Socialism as we see and as we feel it today, in 1959, not 1918, and I hope that in due course another Conference will endorse what they propose."[8]

Most trade unions had then, and still have, rules in their constitutions which commit them to public ownership and/or workers' control.[9] A change in the Party's constitution implied a change in their own. It soon became clear that for this and other reasons many Unions would be unwilling to support a comprehensive reworking of the Labour Party's constitution. Many Unions favoured public ownership in their own industries, and wished to extend it to new sectors. Thus, the miners could see no reason why coal distribution should not be brought under some form of public ownership, as well as the pits themselves. Intermittently calls were to be heard advocating the extension of public ownership to the manufacture of mining machinery. In many other trade unions, the extension of public ownership was at last thinkable.

But in addition, there was a very large group of people who had no desire whatever to extend nationalisation in the immediate future, but who were annoyed by the raising of a question which they regarded as quite irrelevant.

George Brown, soon to be Gaitskell's deputy, summed up the view of this group:

"Gaitskell, quite reasonably, felt that this bit of old-fashioned dogma was part of Labour's out-of-date image, and that far from attracting adherents to the Party it probably put off many people who would otherwise vote Labour. I didn't think it really mattered a damn, one way or the other. But the proposal to amend Clause IV at once aroused all the hostility of those who were really opposed to Gaitskell on defence and all the other matters on which a practical approach to the problems of government contrasted with a doctrinaire approach."[10]

Confronting outright opposition, and surrounded by alienation, Gaitskell came, week by week, to seem more and more isolated. His new broom, far from sweeping clean, was soon to be locked back in the cupboard. By February 1960, *The Times* was able to report a remarkable change, under the arresting headline: "Mr Gaitskell calls for more public ownership".

At a meeting in Nottingham, the Leader surprised his by now sceptical audience by saying:

"For my part, I have never been satisfied with the present frontiers between public and private enterprise. To me it is absurd to think, in the face of the huge capital gains now being made in the private sector, that we can achieve the degree of equality we want without an extension of public ownership.

It's absurd to think that we can overcome the present crisis in town and country planning without more public enterprise — we may even have to go back to some of our old ideas about the ownership of urban land.

It's absurd to think that we can solve our housing problem without more municipal ownership, or create an adequate counterweight to big business without an extension of co-operative ownership.

Above all, we cannot be satisfied with the degree of control over the economy which we now possess. If we are to plan successfully for full employment, more investment, and higher productivity, we shall need to extend the public sector, including more public ownership: most obviously, as we said in our election programme, in the fields of steel and road transport; certainly in water supplies, quite probably in the future, as other problems confront us and the case becomes clearer in other fields as well."[11]

The weight of dissent was gathering, and was becoming the more intense with the growth of the Campaign for Nuclear Disarmament, which threatened to isolate the Labour Party leadership from a very large majority of younger people, including those very members of the middle classes to whom experiments in revisionism had been intended to appeal. A change was inevitable. It seems that Harold Wilson thought that he was responsible for finding the formula which settled this argument (according to his biographer, Ben Pimlott).[12] But that was not the perception of George Brown:

> "The ostensible dispute over Clause IV ended almost in a farce. I thought I saw a way of patching up the differences over Clause IV. I wrote an addition to the traditional Clause IV which I likened in the arguments then to adding the New Testament to the Old Testament. But no amendment was put formally to the Party and so none was ever written into the Party's constitution. Instead the Executive presented its statement to the next Conference, and its statement on Labour's aims was accepted as 'a valuable expression of the aims of the Labour Party in the second half of the twentieth century'."[13]

All this amounted to a rare form of leadership. Seeking to lead his followers away from public ownership, Hugh Gaitskell wound up inciting them to demand more of it. His new text even called for "community power over the commanding heights of the economy", after a judicious amendment by Jennie Lee, using her husband's famous phrase.

George Brown succeeded in one thing: the additional text was frequently referred to as "the new testament", in contra-distinction to the old, delivered by Moses in 1918. But in spite of the contemporary perceptions, the old testament has in fact outlived the new. Few today remember the proclamation of 1960, but all labour members know that Clause IV is written on their membership cards.

Nonetheless, the 1960 statement *was* agreed, and might, in 1995, even seem quite advanced. This is how it read:

> "The following statement adopted in 1960 reaffirms, amplifies and clarifies Party Objects in the light of post-war developments and the historic achievements of the first majority Labour Government.
>
> The British Labour Party is a democratic socialist party. Its central ideal is the brotherhood of man. Its purpose is to make this ideal a reality everywhere.
>
> Accordingly —
> (a) It rejects discrimination on grounds of race, colour or

creed and holds that men should accord to one another equal consideration and status in recognition of the fundamental dignity of Man.

(b) Believing that no nation, whatever its size or power, is justified in dictating to or ruling over other countries against their will, it stands for the right of all peoples to freedom, independence and self-government.

(c) Recognising that international anarchy and the struggle for power between nations must lead to universal destruction, it seeks to build a world order within which all will live in peace. To this end it is pledged to respect the United Nations Charter, to renounce the use of armed force except in self-defence and to work unceasingly for world disarmament, the abolition of all nuclear weapons and the peaceful settlement of international disputes.

(d) Rejecting the economic exploitation of one country by another it affirms the duty of richer nations to assist poorer nations and to do all in their power to abolish poverty thoughout the world.

(e) It stands for social justice, for a society in which the claims of those in hardship or distress come first; where the wealth produced by all is fairly shared among all; where differences in rewards depend not upon birth or inheritance but on the effort, skill and creative energy contributed to the common good; and where equal opportunities exist for all to live a full and varied life.

(f) Regarding the pursuit of material wealth by and for itself as empty and barren, it rejects the selfish, acquisitive doctrines of capitalism, and strives to create instead a socialist community based on fellowship, co-operation and service in which all can share fully in our cultural heritage.

(g) Its aim is a classless society from which all class barriers and false social values have been eliminated.

(h) It holds that to ensure full employment, rising production, stable prices and steadily advancing living standards the nation's economy should be planned and all concentrations of power subordinated to the interests of the community as a whole.

(i) It stands for democracy in industry, and for the right of the workers both in the public and private sectors to full consultation in all the vital decisions of management, especially those affecting conditions of work.

(j) It is convinced that these social and economic objectives can be achieved only through an expansion of common ownership substantial enough to give the community power over the commanding heights of the economy. Common ownership takes varying forms, including state-owned industries and firms, producer and consumer co-operation, municipal ownership and public participation in private concerns. Recognising that both public and private enterprise have a place in the economy it believes that further extension of common ownership should be decided from time to time in the light of these objectives and according to circumstances, with due regard for the views of the workers and consumers concerned.

(k) It stands for the happiness and freedom of the individual against the glorification of the state — for the protection of workers, consumers and all citizens against any exercise of arbitrary power, whether by the state, by private or by public authorities, and it will resist all forms of collective prejudice and intolerance.

(l) As a democratic Party believing that there is no true Socialism without political freedom, it seeks to obtain and to hold power only through free democratic institutions whose existence it has resolved always to strengthen and defend against all threats from any quarter."[14]

As a commonsense statement of the prevailing consensus within the Labour Party in 1960, this declaration is interesting. It tells us where people were at. Indeed, many Labour supporters in 1995 would find it quite remarkably advanced, and certainly less constrictive than subsequent leadership statements have commonly become.

But all the arguments about "full employment", welcome though they are in the desert which has spread across large areas of the British economy since 1979, also reveal the immense gap between the entire Labour Party of 1960 and its socialist forebears. When Webb wrote of "common ownership", this quite explicitly implied the *abolition* of "employment". If all of us shared in the ownership of our enterprise, thought the pioneers, then there would be no "employers", and no employees either.

The Webbs had a special reason to be familiar with this kind of thinking. When they had been writing their famous *History of Trade Unionism*, in 1894, they began with an attempted definition.

> "A trade union, as we understand the term, is a continuous association of wage earners for the purpose of maintaining or improving the conditions of their employment."[15]

But when they re-edited this classic work for students of the Workers' Educational Association, in 1920, they deleted the word "employment", and substituted the term "working lives". They made this change, they said, because they had been accused of assuming that unions had "always contemplated a perpetual continuance of the capitalist or wage-system". No such implication, they insisted, was intended.

It became unfashionable to speak or think of wage-slavery, or what the Guild Socialists called "the bondage of wagery". But this criticism, of the very nature of the employment contract, is a recurrent and insistent strand of the socialist commitment.

We have learnt that there are many perils which attend experiments in social ownership and democratic self-management. Bureaucracy has haunted the socialist movement since its earliest beginnings. That is why it has become necessary to develop a whole panopoly of democratic control mechanisms in order to establish and maintain the principle of democratic accountability.

But no such principle obtains in capitalist industry, even when it remains small in scale and restricted in influence. In the age when multinational corporations extend their reach around the globe, this lack of responsibility becomes a profound social malaise.

Not only socialists are sensitive to the structured inequality of the employment relationship. That is why in the European

Community, the standard description of the participants in industrial relations is "the social partners". That these partners are not equal has been noticed by every trade union in the field. Partnership is not attained by proclaiming it. But the rhetoric implies the need for a different order of things: even when the prospectus is entirely manipulative, false, it signals recognition of the wrongs involved in inequality and domination.

Footnotes

1. Colin Hurry Associates: *Nationalisation: That Survey*, London, 1959. Polling was organised in 129 marginal constituencies, and 41.7 per cent of Labour voters were reported to want "no more nationalisation".
2. Originally a journal of the leftist emigration from Germany, *Socialist Commentary* was reorganised in 1947 by C.A.R. Crosland, Allan Flanders, and Rita Hinden of the Fabian Society.
3. See Richard Fletcher: *Who Were they Travelling With?* in *CIA and the Labour Movement*, Spokesman, 1977.
4. Mark Abrams and Richard Rose: *Must Labour Lose?*, Penguin Books, 1960, pp.12-14.
5. *Ibid.*
6. Fletcher, *op cit*, p.61.
7. Michael Foot: *Aneurin Bevan, 1945-1960*, Davis-Poynter, 1973, p.630 *et seq.*
8. Labour Party: *Annual Conference Report*, 1959.
9. Thus, the TGWU rules include as a main membership commitment the need "to endeavour by all means in their power to control the industries in which their members are engaged,' whilst the first aim of the AEEU is "the control of industry in the interests of the community'. The Foundryworkers' constitution speaks of "developing and extending the co-operative system until a co-operative commonwealth is established which shall labour and produce for the good of all'.
   The NUR sees these perspectives more doctrinally as requiring "the supercession of the capitalist system by a socialist order of society'.
10. George Brown: *In My Way*, Gollancz, 1970.
11. Cited in *Tribune*, 19th February, 1960, p.1.
12. Ben Pimlott: *Harold Wilson*, Harper Collins, 1992, p.238.
13. *Op cit*, p.82.
14. Labour Party: *Annual Conference Report*, 1960.
15. Longman, 1920, Chapter One.

CHAPTER SIX

Why Was This Argument Reopened?

We have seen that there are many similarities between the patterns of argument which developed in 1959 and afterwards, and those of 1994-95.

But there are also very important differences. What underpinned the effort to revise the Labour Party's programme, after the 1959 electoral defeat? The most consistent statement of the "revisionist" view was that of C.A.R. Crosland, in *The Future of Socialism*.[1] Crosland argued that the postwar Labour Government had achieved a major redistribution of personal incomes; a transfer of economic power following the nationalisation of the basic industries; and a transfer of power from management to labour.

The first of these three effects was the best understood, although the statistical evidence was not quite as clear as Crosland thought. His second effect concerned the shift of power occasioned by nationalisation. Here, he was realistic about the fact that the management of nationalised industries might even be less accountable than many private managements. But, he thought, the power of the state had increased, which, for him, was an undoubted plus.

The truth is that the power shift was in fact more complicated than Crosland believed. The nationalisation measures all involved substantial compensation for the original private owners. Since most of the industries concerned were unprofitable, and some were on the brink of actual bankruptcy, their compulsory purchase represented a veritable renewal of the dynamism of capital. Pheonix-like, capital was liberated to seek more profitable areas in which to grow, leaving behind the husks of the derelict industries upon which it had already preyed.

Crosland's third effect was concerned with the beneficial results of full employment.

". . . there has been a decisive movement of power within industry itself from management to labour. This is mainly a consequence of the seller's market for labour created by full employment.

The relative strength of workers and employers does not, of course, depend solely on conditions in the labour market. It depends also on the political balance, the social climate, the degree of organisation of the two sides, and current views about the relation between wages on the one hand, and profits, employment, or the foreign balance on the other. These factors had all changed in a manner favourable to labour even before 1939. Yet the strength of the Unions was still severely limited by large-scale unemployment; and they were obviously, and knew it, the weaker of the two contenders.

The change from a buyer's to a seller's market for labour, however, by transposing at once the interests, and therefore the attitudes, of the two sides, had dramatically altered the balance of power at every level of labour relations.

At the level of the individual worker, the decisive change relates to the question of dismissal. The employee, for whom dismissal before the war was often a sentence of long-term unemployment, can now quickly find a job elsewhere; and he has lost, in consequence, his fear of the sack, and with it his docility. The employer, on the other hand, who before the war could replace a dismissed worker from a long waiting-list of applicants for jobs, may now have difficulty in finding any replacement at all; and he has acquired, in consequence, a reluctance to dismiss, and himself has become more docile. Thus the balance of advantage is reversed, and the result is a transformation of relationships at the shop-floor level.

At the level of the plant or firm, the main change lies in the altered attitude of the two sides towards their ultimate weapons of coercion — the strike and the lockout. With unemployment, the employer can often well afford to ensure a strike or initiate a lockout; the odds in the contest are on his side, while the cost of a stoppage, with stocks often high and market conditions unprofitable, may be relatively minor. But with full employment, the odds are quite different, since the workers can now hold out much longer; while the cost of a stoppage in terms of profits foregone is likely, with stocks perhaps low and a lucrative market demand, to be much greater. The employers' incentive to avoid strikes has thus increased in the same measure as the workers' prospects of winning them; the implications for the balance of power are obvious."[2]

Basing himself on the changes which had been registered in these three areas of social life, Crosland reached the opinion that the initial socialist project had been largely completed. Upon the foundations laid in the years after 1945, he thought, equality could now be established.

Throughout the early postwar years, there had been a barrage of propaganda against equalitarian policies. A mythology arose, claiming that new social provision was redistributing resources to the poor, that full employment was eroding differentials and that the Rentier was indeed withering away, as had been foreseen by J.M. Keynes.

If it is often dangerous to believe your own propaganda, it is even more perilous to believe your opponents'. In these sad later days, however, Crosland might not be blamed for doing so. It was only after the publication of his own work that Richard Titmuss published, in 1962, a magisterial dissection of the official statistics on inequality. He showed how the Inland Revenue had influenced the reporting of incomes, by persuading those who could to subdivide their own large incomes into several smaller ones in favour of all their dependents in order to minimise eligibility for higher rates of tax. He also traced the ploy of splitting large amounts payable in one year into smaller ones dispersed over longer times: this device was also economical of tax liability. Titmuss cast a sharp spotlight on fringe benefits, and showed how far the fashionable talk of a disappearing middle-class was based on the uninquisitive interpretation of very imperfect statistics.[3]

The least that we can say about Crosland's evidence on this matter is that it looked better than it really was. There had been a beneficial but far from swingeing change in the distribution of income which would in fact require persistent governmental action to maintain it. But most subsequent governmental action was intended to reverse it.

His second major change concerned the impact of nationalisation on overall economic policy. We have already commented on this argument. It is obvious that the lack of accountability in nationalised industries implied a need for their democratisation, partly by improving their responsiveness to consumers, and partly by the institution of direct worker involvement in the decision-taking processes. Of course, there was also a case for improving the degree of Parliamentary accountability.

All of these actions would have been consonant with the strict spirit of Clause IV, but none of them were ever effectively considered by Labour leaders, leave alone implemented. It is true that there were some attempts to democratise the administration of the nationalised industries, more than a decade later on. These met with little enthusiasm among the Labour Party establishment, with the important exception of Tony Benn.

We are left with the third major issue: full employment. It is perfectly clear today that the celebrations of this final defeat of unemployment were somewhat premature.

Almost twenty years after his classic statement, Crosland wrote a postscript, called *Socialism Now*.[4] In it, he drew the balance sheet of the six years of Labour Government in which he participated, between 1964 and 1970. "Nobody disputes the central failure of economic policy", he said.

"In 1970, unemployment was higher, inflation more rapid and economic growth slower, than when the Conservatives left office in 1964. The growth performance in particular was lamentable; G.D.P. in real terms rose by an average of only 2.3 per cent a year compared with 3.8 per cent in the previous six years. Growth was consistently sacrificed to the balance of payments, notably to the defence of a fixed and unrealistic rate of exchange.

This central failure bedevilled all the efforts and good intentions of the Labour Government. It constrained public expenditure. It antagonized the Trade Unions and alienated large groups of workers. It killed the National Plan and frustrated policies for improving the industrial structure (though too much was expected both of indicative planning and industrial policy, which are rather marginal influences on economic performance). And it has made it hard for Labour to claim in future — or, rather, it would have done but for the far worse mess which the Tories are making of the economy — that we can manage things more efficiently than they can."[5]

It is not at all clear that the zealous application of Clause IV was responsible for any of these shortcomings. On the contrary, Crosland goes on to list a number of countervailing gains, all of which showed certain improvements in income distribution and in equality of access to education and other services.

What was really going on during this painful experience was that Crosland and some of his colleagues were desperately trying to remain loyal to what they saw as their most binding promise: the pursuit of equality. But effective control over the economy was slipping away, as the power of transnational capital grew and grew. The old modes of national economic control no longer functioned adequately. Changes in fiscal policies commonly did not bite where they were supposed to bite, and even if they did, they failed to create the effects intended.

We shall return to this matter a little later.

At this point in our argument it seems reasonable to conclude that the effort to revise Clause IV of the Labour Party's Constitution in 1959 and 1960 rested on Crosland's three main assumptions about the extent and success of post-war social reform, each of which was largely mistaken.

Of course, some of those who joined the "revisionist" lobby were not motivated by the high principles which animated C.A.R. Crosland. He sought a combination of liberty and equality. Some of the other lobbyists might have settled for something less, such as office or a pension. However, we must take the argument at its strongest, and there is a very great deal of evidence to attest to the sincerity of Crosland

and an important group of his intimates. Unfortunately, the price of equality is eternal vigilance.

What is the difference between this historical discussion, and the present argument? We have seen that inequalities in almost every social dimension have been rapidly increasing, and that unemployment has fundamentally undermined the power of trade unions and the choices of employees in a buyers' market for labour. To restore a sellers' market would be a vast step forward. To consult Richard Titmuss or his pupils in order to frame an effectively redistributive tax policy must, in today's Britain, appear to be a wildly unrealistic, indeed, Utopian effort. There are no good Samaritans on Labour's Front Bench. Public ownership could be restored in a number of services and industries, but the same Front Bench is not only making no new promises, but actively rescinding all the old ones.

How, then, can anyone involved in this surrealist orgy of "realism", speak of "equality"? True, the Labour leadership has circulated a document in which it says it is not speaking of "arithmetic equality".

Amen to that. In every field we are being asked to adjust to discriminatory forms of treatment. We are told that trade unions should seek no special favours. That is to say, that employers are to retain the special favours which they have enjoyed since the beginning of the Thatcher regime. Heavy hints are given to the newspapers that Labour will pursue every possibility of cutting taxes, rather than deploy them to help the poor. The resultant equality will certainly not be arithmetical. It will be comprehensively Orwellian. All animals will be equal, but some will be considerably more equal than others. The animals will look "from pig to man, and from man to pig, and from pig to man again". But already it will be impossible, or at any rate politically incorrect, to say which is which.

Respect for C.A.R. Crosland demands that we recognise that this kind of equality is nothing whatever to do with that which motivated his political life. There is a real chasm between the two ideals of equality, and between the two constitutional debates.

How has it come about that a national Labour movement could be so comprehensively emptied of spirit and commitment?

One should not be tempted to recriminate about the low cultural level of some of the leading participants in this discussion. The question is not how did certain not very resonant arguments come to be advanced: it is, how did they come to the front in a Party representing a vast population suffering unprecedented hardships and indeed miseries, and yet consisting of millions of people with high levels of education, skill and ability?

There is a very simple answer. Multinational capital has largely annulled national democracy. National parliaments may still squabble about the fruits of office, and they may still legislate on second order questions. But the vast macro-economic decisions cannot be taken in national chancelleries or monitored in State Parliaments, and indeed are normally not taken at all. Multinational capital has succeeded in establishing a free range over which it marauds with impunity. Much of this range is comprehensively deregulated. The Keynesian levers which enabled Crosland to aspire to the control of social policy through the British Government's machinery of redistribution will not be reconnected until we create levels of transnational democracy which can match and contend with the economic power centres.

Geological shifts in the real power structures were largely unremarked by Labour's policy makers throughout the 60s and most of the 70s. The result was increasing frustration, as the political machine began to malfunction in more and more tiresome and unpredictable ways.

The most important lessons of these experiences were drawn by Stuart Holland, who had been a personal assistant to Harold Wilson in the traumatic years of his first administration. In an important book, *The Socialist Challenge*,[6] Holland developed the fundamental analysis which lay at the base of the alternative economic strategy, which was to be embraced by the whole of the left, throughout the 1970s, and even later.

Holland showed that the failure of Keynesian management techniques to deliver controlled growth in Britain was part of a wider change which resulted from the growth of multinational corporations, able individually to circumvent and together to block national governmental policies over a wide range of matters. Between the macro and micro levels of economic analysis, Holland argued, we needed to see that there had arisen a *meso*-level represented by the giant corporations, which could subvert or nullify many of the decisions taken by macro-economic planners. Since giant companies accounted for a greater and greater proportion of world trade, and since much of that trade was now internal to specific corporations, devices like that of transfer pricing enabled corporations to avoid national taxation rules at will. The prices of transferred components could be charged at wholly fictional levels, in order to remove company resources from one area to another, without hindrance. Transnational subsidiaries would be favoured for straightforward company reasons, even when national trade balances were running adversely.

In this way, too, big companies would play the exchanges, and develop responses to the next level of state management intervention. As they became less and less capable of controlling their national economies by conventional fiduciary means, governments were forced into the position of competitive borrowing in order to maintain the parities of their currencies. A Dutch auction of interest rates followed, reinforcing inflationary pressures.

What was then left of the democratic socialist project? With great skill and imagination, parts of it could still be recuperated at the national level, provided the new conditions were understood. However, the main weight of economic decision-making had evaded direct national controls, and could only be met and matched at an appropriate transnational level. At the same time, of course, transnational political powers were far too weak to afford a readymade framework to a modern Crosland, seeking to manage the world of giant multinationals on broad Keynesian principles. National powers were eroding, and national institutions were crumbling with them.

True, a beginning of recuperation could be envisaged with the developing institutions of the European Community, and as those institutions evolved towards full-fledged European Union, it became at least thinkable that a co-ordinated policy of redistribution and social intervention might once again render renewed welfare politics viable for the medium term. But the new economy is increasingly global, so that even the European Union cannot match the economic institutions point by point, and evolve all the counterpart mechanisms of macro-economic control which had become so indispensable to the Crosland generation.

The evolution of a single currency might in time put European institutions at the fulcrum in negotiations to recreate a new international economic and monetary order. Social considerations might then recover some of their older priority.

But in the meantime, socialists in different countries would need greatly improved forms of co-operation among themselves. Without these, there would be no valid long term national strategies, no honest joint actions, and no realisable combined and convergent policies to advance the interests of our constituency: the working population, the unemployed, the poor, and the forgotten people of Europe. Separately, the national roads diverged in one direction into sterile dogmas, and in the other to a sickeningly conformist opportunism.

But the real choice, which is to work together, to transcend frontiers and barriers, leads to new possibilities of advance, towards that long-delayed world in which "the free development of each is the condition of the free development of all".

Footnotes

1. C.A.R. Crosland: *The Future of Socialism*, Jonathan Cape, 1956.
2. *Op cit*, p.30, *et seq.*
3. Richard M. Titmuss: *Income Distribution and Social Change: A Study in Criticism*, Allen and Unwin, 1962.
4. Anthony Crosland: *Socialism Now*, Jonathan Cape, 1974.
5. *Op cit*, p.18.
6. Quartet, 1975.

CHAPTER SEVEN

Why Labour Should Fly Its Own Colours

with a contribution by Clement Attlee

Aneurin Bevan once explained the political question which dominated his life. It was: "Where does power lie in this particular state of Great Britain, and how can it be attained by the workers?" He described how he followed through the pursuit of power to Parliament, and ultimately to the Cabinet. Power, he discovered, was a will-o'-the-wisp.

A modern Bevan would find a modern Cabinet very much reduced in its influence. Contrary to certain rumours its scope is not decisively restricted by the extension of regulations agreed in Brussels. The overpowering restriction comes from the fact that the big economic entities have escaped from the political process, leaving behind a broken shell, parts of which are to be found in Westminster, and parts in Brussels or elsewhere. Within the remnants of the shell, certain changes can be negotiated, provided they offer no fundamental challenges to the extraordinary powers. That is the problem which we need to overcome. It amounts to nothing less than the reinvention of democracy, and whilst it needs to be done at the European level, since we already have some of the fundamental groundwork linkages there, it needs simultaneously to be done at both the national and regional or local levels.

Such a regeneration can involve us in alliances. But alliances which are not directed to this purpose of democratic recovery and social renewal will merely frustrate and disappoint their participants. Is it in pursuit of such inevitably disappointing alliances that the Labour leadership has now set out on the abandonment of Clause IV? We have seen that Clause IV came into being as a conscious act to separate Labour supporters from the ancient influence of the Liberals. This separation was a complex political operation. Mainstream Labour, as we have already insisted, rightly had no desire at all to separate itself from Liberal commitments to individual freedom, and to the goal of self-realisation preached by the more consistent Liberal philosophers throughout the nineteenth century. But the Labour men and women had concluded that such freedoms were not open, or rather, were actually *closed*, to the whole class of employees, who were deprived not only of political rights, but also of the economic space in which to develop to the limits of their talents, and realise their own capacities. Common ownership of land and capital was the answer to private ownership, and it was intended to redress the fundamental inequity: that Labour was employed by capital. Instead capital would need to be employed by Labour. Liberal entrepreneurs did not think this was a good idea.

Today, there is ground for believing that what is at stake is not a formal alliance, but an effort to shift the political ground, moving the Labour Party across into Liberal territory and displacing its present occupants. But who will then minister to the needs of Labour's forgotten millions?

To annul Clause IV might well annul the dividing line between New Labour and surviving Liberalism. But it will not resolve the ancient problem of subordination, in which capital rules Labour, rather than Labour employing capital. In the confusion which envelops modern politics, it is true that there are many individual Liberals who are alive to this problem and would cheerfully embrace what many of us regard as Socialist solutions to it. Perhaps this is why some Labour supporters have developed the idea of "a popular front of the mind".

But the mind is the very last place in which to seek such an alignment. Political thinking needs to be clear, and the necessary clarity to solve our problems will not be found in a pot of fudge. Labour will never win anything real until it knows how to recreate the political conditions for full employment.

Undoubtedly the Labour leadership is influenced by the idea of a popular front, which it inherits from its advisers, some of whom hail from the former Communist Party grouped around *Marxism Today*, and a number of whom are recent leading members of the Social Democratic Party, who in turn were drawn towards *Marxism Today* and its seminars.

The modern popular front, we must hasten to say, does not necessarily take the form of a formal alliance between Liberals and Labour. That is why Ben Pimlott has situated it "in the mind". It may mean that Tony Blair's superior ideas invade the brain of Paddy Ashdown, and render him amenable to intense co-operation. Or the process might develop in an opposite direction: but the result would still be likely to constitute a considerable let down. There isn't that much in either mind to remain acceptable, leave alone "popular" for very many minutes.

The problem is that none of these political forces is confronting the major question, which is the reconstruction of democracy at an effective level, where the power of the people can reimpose its controls on our economy which has escaped from political space. The overpowering reason why this must be done is that full employment cannot be recovered without a recovery of democratic power.

The provenance of the popular front idea is not so good. It began as an arm of Communist international policy, once the divisions of the German left had allowed the rise of Hitler in Germany. Initial experiments in France and Spain were generalised into campaigns throughout the surviving European democracies. In what follows we reproduce the writings of Clement Attlee on the British variant of the strategy. Attlee's strictures retain their validity, and are a classic statement of the values of mainstream Labour.

The original idea of the popular front was that Socialist and non-Socialist Parties should co-operate to prevent the encroachment of fascism. Such an alliance cannot be on today's agenda, since those who favour capitalism do not really wish to extend the scope of Government in order to bring that economy under public, leave alone democratic, control. Fascism may disrupt the present order, but big capitalists don't want the big government that goes with it.*

But in any case, popular fronts developed, and after the Second World War, several of them took power. True, they usually required the help of the Soviet army. In Hungary,

---

*This does not mean they won't accommodate, if the socialists remain bankrupt of convincing solutions to the present crisis, and the ultra-right learns how to profit from the resultant mess. Watch Mr Berlusconi!

Prime Minister Rakosi developed the second stage of popular front theory under the rubric "salami tactics". First you came to power, and then you cut and cut again, in thin slices, until the "unreliable" forces no longer existed. All over Eastern Europe, popular fronts turned into cemeteries.

To a generation which has seen the fall of the Berlin Wall, perhaps these ideas might seem somewhat suspect. But for certain aspirants to power, they retain an appeal, it seems.

All these are very tricky arguments. Some who seek for a popular front seek in the best traditions of Rakosi to dissemble their intentions. Others are seeking a thorough realignment of politics and yet appreciate the great difficulties which are involved in keeping their own followers on side.

The Labour Party and affiliated organisations should avoid all this kind of manoeuvres. We need to ask ourselves what goals we seek to achieve, and then to decide what impediments stand in our way. Since we do share commitments with old socialists and old social democrats like Crosland, we can all agree that the right to work is basic to the establishment of a free society. But the right to work will not be restored solely by national action, any more than it can be regained in one borough or one village. (Village and borough action is not at all dispensable, however: without it no-one will find the focus required to bring change.)

Can the framework for a comrehensive socialist movement in Europe be constructed? Could a British Labour Government help remove some of the major blocks to full employment policy? What extensions of public enterprise at local and regional levels might help within such a framework? These are the practical questions which we should address, and the destruction of Clause IV would give no help to this process. We shall have to return to it, once we have secured our intellectual inheritance. The present debate needs to identify the precise scope for the extension of public job-creating services and activities, so that people can see that this is a commitment vital to their lives into the twenty-first century, not a sentimental attachment.

*   *   *

"We cannot administer capitalism because we don't believe in it!"Clement Attlee

The last time that there was a serious prospect of an electoral alliance between Labour and the Liberals, it took the form of calls for a "popular front". Clement Attlee had recently been elected leader of the Labour Party. This is how he evaluated the project, in his contribution to the Left Book Club*: 'The Labour Party in Perspective'.*

The Labour Party stands for such great changes in the economic and social structure that it cannot function successfully unless it obtains a majority which is prepared to put its principles into practice. Those principles are so far-reaching that they affect every department of the public services and every phase of policy. The plain fact is that a Socialist Party cannot hope to make a success of administering the Capitalist system because it does not believe in it. This is the fundamental objection to all the proposals that are put forward for the formation of a Popular Front in this country.

There are many people who suggest that what is required at the present time is the formation of an alliance between all the Left Wing forces in order to get rid of the present Government. The argument is based sometimes on the need for getting through certain urgent reforms in home affairs, sometimes, and perhaps more frequently, on the plea that at all events all can unite on a common policy in foreign affairs, and that on this basis it would be possible to rally a majority in this country for what is vaguely called a Left Government. Many people stress the purely negative attitude — that is to say, the urgent need of getting rid of the present administration before, through their feeble and dishonest policy, they allow the world to be plunged into war. Others believe that it is possible to form a short-term policy to which the various Left Wing groups would give their adhesion, and that upon this basis electoral arrangements could be made which would ensure a majority.

I would not myself rule out such a thing as an impossibility in the event of the imminence of a world crisis. It might on a particular occasion be the lesser of two evils, but it is worth while examining these proposals in some detail, because they have an appeal to many who do not in my view look far enough ahead.

I will first deal with the purely negative proposal which considers that the really vital thing is the extrusion from power of the present Government. I should be the last person to underrate the importance of this, but the overthrow of the present Government means its replacement by another. You cannot simply leave a vacuum.

A majority of heterogeneous composition returned on a negative policy of turning the Government out, with a clear foreign policy but no programme for home affairs, would not last more than a few weeks. Even where foreign affairs overshadow the political scene, the day to day work of a Government is mainly concerned with administration and legislation on internal affairs. The essential support that a Government needs is not for a few major issues, but for the ordinary common round and daily task. The first essential for a Government which has to work through the House of Commons is command over time. More things are lost by delay than by open opposition. The elaborate machinery of the Whips Office, and the discipline imposed on the supporters of a Government, are essential if it is to function at all. This discipline, although enforced by pains and penalties, by hopes of reward and by the fear of dissolution, depends in the last resort far more on a realisation by the members of the relative importance of particular issues. The discipline imposed by membership of a party not only in the House of Commons, but in constituency party work, is a reflection of a general appraisement of the value of the attainment of certain aims, and a willingness to subordinate the particular points on which the individual feels keenly to the general sense of the Party. It is, in fact, the acceptance of the fundamental principle of democracy — majority rule.

It has never been easy to obtain this discipline in parties of the Left. Parties of the Right tend to contain fewer individualities, while their members in this country have been drilled by the nature of their upbringing to the acceptance of what they would term the team spirit. Parties of the Left tend to be composed of enthusiasts for particular reforms who hope by joining with others to achieve their aims, and of men and women who have through their individuality come to the front, rather than those who by the possession of wealth or position have drifted into politics. Thus the Liberal Party always tended to be fissiparous. It always included in its ranks a number of what are called impolitely "cranks" — that is to say, enthusiasts for various good causes. The party was kept together by the large body of persons who were traditional Liberals, or perhaps even without any market convictions except an interest in politics and a desire to make a career.

In the Labour Party, the Trade Union element serves as the solid core of disciplined membership. The loyalty to majority decisions, which is the foundation of industrial action, takes the place of what is called among Conservatives the team spirit, while long training in the responsibilities of Trade Union work has induced a habit of mind which realises the practical necessity for compromise in non-essentials. A further link which makes for united action is the common faith in Socialism which inspires the members. There are, however, always a few who, while convinced Socialists, have as their main incentive devotion to some particular reform. Their enthusiasm for their own special cause is apt at times to make them lose their sense of proportion. There are also, naturally, some members whose fervent desire for the achievement of their ideals makes them impatient of the delays and partial successes which are inevitable in working through the methods of parliamentary democracy.

The experience of the two Labour Governments showed how difficult it was for many of these to accept the compromises inseparable from all Government, but particularly from a Government in a minority. There was needed to give the experiment the degree of success which it attained the full force of party loyalty and of devotion to the cause of Socialism.

But if there is to be an election resulting in the return of a majority consisting of several minorities united only on a negative, the Government will be intolerably weak. If the groups are in themselves strong and coherent, it may be possible, by the inclusion of leaders drawn from all of them, to obtain a fairly consistent support, but at best the battle will only be transferred from the floor of the House and party meetings to the Cabinet Room. The larger the party the greater its sense of responsibility; the smaller the group the more irresponsible. The largest party becomes at once the prisoner of the minority groups, which put all the pressure they can to ensure decisions in the sense which they desire . . .

Many of these objections apply equally to the suggestion that there should be a positive programme to which all organisations on the Left should adhere. It is thought that many Liberals might accept a limited programme of certain specific items calculated to be carried through within the life of one Parliament, and that upon this basis a Left Government might be achieved at an early date. It is thought that there is a large body of Left opinion which, while unwilling to commit itself to Socialism, is yet prepared to accept a considerable instalment of the Socialist programme. It is commonly suggested that enough work for one Parliament could be found without going beyond the limits which would repel adherents of the Capitalist system.

It must be admitted that there is considerable strength of opinion in support of this proposition, and I think that there is ground for the view that there are many in this country who are prepared to go a long way with the Labour Party while not prepared to take the plunge and join any affiliated organisation. It is, therefore, worth while examining this proposition.

The first question that arises is as to the limits of the programme which would be acceptable. I find that the proposition often reduces itself to this — that if the Labour Party would drop its Socialism and adopt a Liberal platform, many Liberals would be pleased to support it. I have heard it said more than once that if Labour would only drop its policy of nationalisation everyone would be pleased, and it would soon obtain a majority.

I am convinced that it would be fatal for the Labour Party to form a Popular Front on any such terms. It may be possible in other countries, but not in this. I have stated above that Socialists cannot make Capitalism work. The 1929 experiment demonstrated this. No really effective steps could be taken to deal with the economic crisis, because any attempt to deal with fundamentals brought opposition from the Liberals. Labour men who saw clearly the need for dealing with causes had to try to deal with results. The amount that could be extracted for the workers from a Capitalist system was limited. When this limit had been reached, failure was bound to ensue. I admit that the experiment was not made under fair conditions. The Party was handicapped by the conditions of the time, which demanded drastic measures, and by its leading personnel, who had surrendered their minds to Capitalism long before they sold their bodies.

Therefore any such short programme to be acceptable to Socialists must contain measures which will take the country a long way on the road to the desired goal. It must contain a big instalment of nationalisation. The subjects of nationalisation must be not those about which there is little controversy, because they are not vital, but those which are really vital for the transformation of society and are called for in the national interest. I shall indicate later what I believe these to be, but I do not know how far it would be possible for any large number of Liberals to accept them.

Next, there must be a development of the control of the community over trade and industry, which runs counter to the shibboleths of individualism. I do not underrate the value of the suspicion of bureaucracy which the Liberals exhibit. It is, indeed, necessary that Socialists should import into the structure of the society which they are building what is valid in Liberalism, but I have the impression that Liberal elements in a Popular Front Government would baulk at necessary controls.

With this there must be a steady pressure exerted through the medium of the Budget, wage standards, social services, etc., towards a more equalitarian society. I return to the point which I made above — that in the carrying on of a Government it is all-round support that is required. A Socialist

Government must inform its whole administration with the Socialist ideal. All its Ministers must be conscious of the goal to which they are steering the ship of State. It is just here that I see the crux of the situation. In a Popular Front the Socialist elements are definitely out to replace Capitalism by Socialism. They work with that aim in view all the time. If, on the other hand, they have colleagues or supporters whose conscious aim is the preservation of Capitalism, there cannot possibly be harmony.

There are those who will say that this is a playing with words; that "We are all Socialists now"; that there is no absolute Socialism or Capitalism; that it is all a matter of degree and so forth. I cannot accept this. Socialism to me is not just a piece of machinery or an economic system, but a living faith translated into action. I desire the classless society, and the substitution of the motive of service for that of competition. I must, therefore, differ in my outlook from the man who still clings to the present system. Even though we agree that, say, the mines should be nationalised, we disagree with the end in view and with the reason for our action. He regards the mining industry as an exception to the general way he wishes to carry on industry. He thinks that owing to the history and conditions of the industry it had better be nationalised, but he still regards it as a profit-making undertaking. I, on the other hand, conceive it as a basic activity of the community for providing certain necessary needs, and as but the first of many services which must undergo a transformation.

CHAPTER EIGHT

Common Ownership

Now that the Labour Party is reassessing its Constitution, and wondering whether, or how, to revise its famous Clause IV, on common ownership, some voices are to be heard asking what it all really means. The effort to find out leads us back into our history.

In a remarkably rich little book, *Keywords*, Raymond Williams focused his mind on the complex knot of ambiguities which attach to the misleadingly simple word "common" in English.

The Latin root for this word is *communis*. As Williams points out, two alternative (and indeed opposing) derivations have been offered for this. One gives the Latin *com-*, meaning "together", with *munis*, the Latin for "under obligation". The other gives *com-* with *unus*, meaning "one". So we move from common to community, which Williams tracks back to the 14th century for its meaning as "an organised body of people".

Clause IV, drafted by the Fabian founder Sidney Webb, speaks of the "common ownership" of the means of production, distribution and exchange. This clearly relates to a long tradition of *commonwealth*. Out pops the ambiguity: the community as one gives us a commonwealth of all society. The community as being under obligation gives us the commons as commoners, or the lowly, versus the lords and nobility, and renders "commonwealth" a subversive concept, sharing out that which had previously been expropriated by the rich.

Williams picked up a very interesting example of the evolving usage of this word. During the Civil War in England members of the parliamentary army "refused to be called common soldiers" and insisted instead that they were "private" soldiers. That is to say, they were rejecting subordination and the derogatory use of the word "common" as meaning "low" or "vulgar". A private soldier was his own man, motivated by his own chosen ends. He was fighting for objectives for which he had freely enlisted himself so that his cause was his personal choice. But Williams hastens to complete the paradox: these soldiers had recruited themselves to battle for, on behalf of, *the commons* and indeed they went on to create a commonwealth. In the New Model Army, a private soldier was somebody, because he was devoting himself to a common cause. Subsequently a hierarchic army has stripped away this disruptive significance, and reduced the word private to its modern sense: a description of the lowest ranker.

When Sidney Webb carefully chose his words for the Labour Party's constitutional draft, there were a number of possible names for a very similar concept. Marxists had long insisted that social production should be brought under social control. Industry could be socialised, or collectivised. The workers in it could control it, manage it, participate in it, or own it. Elaborate social proposals already existed for each of these variants and they were not at all reduceable to a single root. But "common" ownership could pull off this trick and another, at precisely the same time. It could lead back into a long tradition, a continuity of hope and high aspiration.

Nineteenth century writers had made much of *Commonweal*, and indeed William Morris had produced a journal of that name in which he first published his novella, *A Dream of John Ball*.

This was freely derived from Froissart, who had told John Ball's story in his *Chronicles*, four hundred years earlier.

> "This priest used often on Sundays after mass, when the people were coming out of the church, to go into the cloister and preach, and assembling the people about him, would say this:
>
> 'My good people, things cannot go well in England, nor ever shall, till everything be made common, and there are neither villeins nor gentlemen, but we shall all be united

together, and the lords shall be no greater masters than ourselves.'"

William Morris was, of course, a Victorian Romantic, and recruited the imagined medieval past to help him offer his own mordant commentary on the evils of modern industrialism. But self-educated English working men were listening, and not only to socialist evangelists like Morris himself. Many of them struggled to make sense of the new sixpenny editions of Sir Thomas More's *Utopia*. Some parts were more easily accessible than others:

"For the wise man did easily foresee, that this is the one and only way to the wealth of the community, if equality of all things should be brought in and established. Which I think is not possible to be observed, where every man's goods be proper and peculiar to himself. For where every man under certain titles and pretences draweth and plucketh to himself as much as he can, and so a few divide among themselves all the riches that there is, be there never so much abundance and store, there to the residue is left lack and poverty. And for the most part it chanceth that this latter sort is more worthy to enjoy that state of wealth, than the other be; because the rich men be covetous, crafty, and unprofitable: on the other part, the poor be lowly, simple, and by their daily labour more profitable to the common wealth than to themselves.

Thus I do fully persuade myself, that no equal and just distribution of things can be made; nor that perfect wealth shall ever be among men; unless this property be exiled and banished. But so long as it shall continue, so long shall remain among the most and best part of men the heavy and inequitable burden of poverty and wretchedness."

At the end of the nineteenth century, memories of Thomas More were warm in the Catholic Church, when Cardinal Manning was reaching out to the poor, and to the London dockers and their ragged followers in the epoch-shaping strike of 1889.

But the Protestant tradition was also carried forward in the cheap editions which some of the newly educated working people of the late Victorian age were reading.

William Tyndale's sermon against the Mammon of Unrighteousness was resurrected from the archives of 1528, and brought by cheap print before a completely different audience:

> ". . . First, *mammon* is an Hebrew word, and signifies riches and temporal goods, and namely, all superfluity, and all that is above necessity, and that which is required unto our necessary uses, wherewith a man may help another without undoing or hurting himself; for Hamon, in the Hebrew speech, signifies a multitude or abundance, or many, and there hence cometh mahamon, or mammon, abundance of plenteousness of goods or riches.
>
> Secondarily, it is called unrighteous mammon, not because it is got unrighteously, or with usury, for of unrighteous gotten goods can no man do good works, but ought to restore them home again . . .
>
> But singularly before God it is called unrighteous mammon, because it is not bestowed and ministered unto our neighbour's need . . ."

We can hear this voice, echoing down the centuries. It cries out in the tracts of Gerrard Winstanley, in 1649, saying "speak not of mine and thine, but *ours*". It raises its call again in the work of the Quaker, John Bellars. And it is to be heard in full shout among the Chartists, the Owenites, and their successors in the co-operative and Labour Movements.

The socialist movement on behalf of which Webb sought to lobby and bring influence to bear was compounded of many strands, some of which clearly conflicted with one another. Webb was the interpreter of trade unions, and the expositor of local government, prosaic and secular activities both. But just as non-conformity fed its influence into the Independent Labour Party, so the representatives of unskilled labourers in the new unions drew on passionate support from the Catholic Church. And all the time, the Church of England was working through its settlements, teaching and learning from the new socialist schools which shaped the early politics of the 20th century.

The ideal of "Common" ownership signals a profound debt to these influences, as well as a promise of future reform. Will individualism and the pursuit of self-interest serve us as well if they become moral guidelines for the twenty-first century?

CHAPTER NINE

Witnesses for Common Ownership

In 1647, a major debate took place in Putney church. It was to mark a key moment in the course of the English Revolution. The Army Council deliberated upon proposals for an agreement of the people, which the agitators in the army had advanced. This Army Council included the agitators. A long, powerful debate challenged the idea that the right to vote should only go to men of property.

The Putney debates

Mr Pettus *[Maximilian Petty]*: We judge, that all inhabitants that have not lost their birthright should have an equal voice in elections.

Rainsborough: I desired that those that had engaged in it, for really I think that the poorest he that is in England hath a life to live as the greatest he; and therefore truly, sir, I think it's clear, that every man that is to live under a government ought first by his own consent to put himself under that government; and I do think that the poorest man in England is not at all bound in a strict sense to that government that he hath not had a voice to put himself under; and I am confident that, when I have heard the reasons against it, that something will be said to answer those reasons, insomuch that I should doubt whether I was an Englishman or no, that should doubt of these things.

Ireton: That's this.

Give me leave to tell you, that if you make this the rule, I think you must fly for refuge to an absolute natural right, and you must deny all civil right; and I am sure it will come to that in the consequence. This, I perceive, is pressed as that which is so essential and due, the right of the people of this kingdom, and as they are the people of this kingdom, distinct and divided from other people, as that we must for this right lay aside all other considerations . . . I think that no person hath a right to an interest or share in the disposing of the affairs of the kingdom, and in determining or choosing those that shall determine what laws we shall be ruled by here, no person hath a right to this that hath not a permanent fixed interest in this kingdom.

*   *   *

Gerrard Winstanley, *the leader of the diggers in the heroic days of the English Revolution, wrote the* New Law of Righteousnesse *in January 1649.*

Ours, not mine or thine

. . . Let all men say what they will, so long as such are Rulers as call the Land theirs, upholding this particular propriety of *Mine* and *Thine*; the common-people shall never have their liberty, nor the Land ever [be] freed from troubles, oppressions and complainings; by reason whereof the Creator of all things is continually provoked. O thou proud selfish governing *Adam*, in this land called *England!* Know that the cries of the poor, whom thou layeth heavy oppressions upon, is heard . . .

. . . Therefore you dust of the earth, that are trod under foot, you poor people, that makes both scholars and rich men your oppressors by your labours. Take notice of your privilege, the Law of Righteousnesse is now declared.

All the men and women in *England*, are all children of this Land, and the earth is the Lord's, not particular men's that claims a proper interest in it above others, which is the devil's power.

But be it so, that some will say. This is my Land, and call such and such a parcel of Land his own interest; Then saith the Lord, let such an one labour that parcel of Land by his own hands, none helping him: for whosoever shall help that man to labour his proper earth, as he calls it for wages, the hand of the Lord shall be upon such labourers; for they lift up flesh above the spirit, by their labours, and so hold the Creation still under bondage.

Therefore if the rich will still hold fast this propriety of *Mine and Thine*, let them labour their own land with their own hands. And let the common-people, that are the gatherings together of Israel from under that bondage, and that say the earth is ours, not mine, let them labour together, and eat bread together upon the Commons, Mountains, and Hills.

For as the enclosures are called such a man's Land, and such a man's Land; so the Commons and Heath, are called the common-people's, and let the world see who labours the earth in righteousnesse, and . . . let them be the people that shall inherit the earth. Whether they that hold a civil propriety, saying, *This is mine*, which is selfish, devilish and destructive to the Creation, or those that hold a common right, saying, *The earth is ours*, which lifts up the Creation from bondage.

*   *   *

Robert Owen *tried everything. An outstanding entrepreneur, he introduced the most advanced reforms into his mills. But he came to the conclusion that the whole system of capitalism had to be changed before his ideals could be realised. This text is from March 1834, at the height of struggles of Owenite trade unionism.*

The capitalist system
This great truth which I have now to declare to you, is, that 'the system on which all the nations of the world are acting is founded in gross deception, in the deepest ignorance or in a mixture of both. That, under no possible modifications of the principles on which it is based, can it ever produce good to man; but that, on the contrary, its practical results must ever be to produce evil continually' — and, consequently, that no really intelligent and honest individual can any longer support it; for, by the constitution of this system, it unavoidably encourages and upholds, as it ever has encouraged and upheld, hypocrisy and deception of every description, and discouraged and opposed truth and sincerity, whenever truth and sincerity were applied permanently to improve the condition of the human race. It encourages and upholds national vice and corruption to an unlimited extent; whilst to an equal degree it discourages national virtue and honesty. The whole system has not one

redeeming quality; its very virtues, as they are termed, are vices of great magnitude. Its charities, so called, are gross acts of injustice and deception. Its instructions are to rivet ignorance in the mind and, if possible, render it perpetual. It supports, in all manner of extravagance, idleness, presumption, and uselessness; and oppresses, in almost every mode which ingenuity can devise, industry, integrity and usefulness. It encourages superstition, bigotry and fanaticism; and discourages truth, commonsense and rationality. It generates and cultivates every inferior quality and base passion that human nature can be made to receive; and has so disordered all the human intellects, that they have become universally perplexed and confused, so that man has no just title to be called a reasonable and rational being. It generates violence, robbery and murder, and extols and rewards these vices as the highest of all virtues. Its laws are founded in gross ignorance of individual man and of human society; they are cruel and unjust in the extreme, and, united with all the superstitions in the world, are calculated only to teach men to call that which is pre-eminently true and good, false and bad; and that which is glaringly false and bad, true and good . . .

In consequence of the dire effects of this wretched system upon the whole of the human race, the population of Great Britain — the most advanced of modern nations in the acquirement of riches, power and happiness — has created and supports a theory and practice of government which is directly opposed to the real well-being and true interests of every individual member of the empire, whatever may be his station, rank or condition — whether subject or sovereign. And so enormous are the increasing errors of this system now become, that, to uphold it the government is compelled, day by day, to commit acts of the grossest cruelty and injustice, and to call such proceedings laws of justice and of Christian mercy.

Under this system, the idle, the useless and the vicious govern the population of the world; whilst the useful and the truly virtuous, as far as such a system will permit men to be virtuous, are by them degraded and oppressed . . .

Men of industry, and of good and virtuous habits! This is the last state to which you ought to submit; nor would I advise you to allow the ignorant, the idle, the presumptuous and the vicious, any longer to lord it over the well-being, the lives and happiness, of yourselves and families, when, by *three days* of such idleness as constitutes the whole of their lives, you would for ever convince each one of these mistaken individuals that you now possess the power to compel *them* at once to become the abject slaves, and the oppressed portion of society which they have hitherto made *you.*

*   *   *

The Pioneer, *at Ilkeston, espoused the cause of the Owenite unions, and persistently reported the extraordinary events during the Derby Turnouts, in which workers of all trades sought to establish co-operative production. Senex wrote this stirring piece on 14th June 1834.*

Wages
I would banish the word *wages* from the language, and consign it, with the word slavery, to histories and dictionaries. *Wages* is a term of purchase; it means the piecemeal purchase of your blood, and bones, and brains, at weekly payments; it is the present name for the *Saturday's market price of man, woman, and child*!

*   *   *

The Origins of Inequality
The first man who, having enclosed a piece of land, thought of saying 'This is mine' and found people simple enough to believe him, was the true founder of civil society. How many crimes, wars, murders; how much misery and horror the human race would have been spared if someone had pulled up the stakes and filled in the ditch and cried out to his fellow men: 'Beware of listening to this impostor. You are lost if you forget that the fruits of the earth belong to everyone and that the earth itself belongs to no one!'
Jean Jacques Rousseau

*   *   *

The Chartist leader, **James Bronterre O'Brien**, *came from the radical wing of the movement for universal manhood suffrage. The first national petition was signed by 1,280,000 people. Here O'Brien draws some important lessons from America . . .*

Of human slavery

In the principal states of Europe and America, in our colonies generally, and indeed in most modern countries called 'civilized', wages-slavery is the normal condition of the labouring classes. This latter kind of slavery is *caeteris paribus*, more or less intensely severe according to the degree of perfection to which civilization is carried. Thus in our limited kingdom, which is accounted the most civilized country in the world, wages-slavery is attended with greater hardships, and subject to more privations and casualties, than anywhere else. Nowhere else do we find employment so precarious; nowhere else such multitudes of people over-worked at one time and totally destitute of employment at other times; nowhere else do we see such masses of the population subsisting upon pittances wholly inadequate to sustain human beings in health and strength; nowhere else do we find gaols and workhouses so overcrowded; nowhere else do we hear of whole districts depopulated by famine; nor of upwards of 1,500,000 out of eight millions of people being cut off by actual starvation and forced expatriation in the course of twelve months, as has happened in Ireland in our own times. All this too we find to be contemporaneous and in juxta-position with granaries, warehouses, and shops teeming with a superabundance of the choicest produce of all climes — with cries of over-production and glutted markets ringing in our ears wherever we pass — and with the most opulent and numerous aristocracy, territorial and commercial that was ever known to be congregated in any country of seven times the extent — to say nothing of a still more numerous middle class . . .

*   *   *

George Bernard Shaw *was invited to give a lecture to the industrial remuneration conference in 1885. The great dramatist was asked to make no criticism of any particular class; hence his defence of burglars . . .*

Understanding the burglars

Mr George Bernard Shaw (Fabian Society) said: . . . On the general question of the welfare of the community no reasonable defence could be advanced of the existence of any class that consumed the product of the national industry without rendering any service to the nation in return. It was the desire of the President that nothing should be said that might give pain to particular classes. He was about to refer to a modern class — the burglars; but if there was a burglar present, he begged him to believe that he cast no reflection upon his profession (laughter), and that he was not unmindful of his great skill and enterprise; his risks — so much greater than those of the most speculative capitalist, extending as they did to risk of liberty and life (laughter); his abstinence; or, finally, of the greater number of people to whom he gave employment, including criminal attorneys, policemen, turn-keys, gaolers, builders of gaols, and, it might be, the hangman. He did not wish to hurt the feelings of shareholders, who drew interest year after year, and, if they sold out, expected to get the original investment back again, or of landlords, who did nothing for the rents they received, any more than he wished to pain the burglars. He would merely point out that all three inflicted on the community an injury of precisely the same nature (laughter). We must stop this state of things before we could reform our present condition. It would be said that to expropriate the landlord and capitalist would be unjust, immoral, confiscation, and so forth; but the truth was that it was absolutely immoral to allow them any longer to confiscate daily the labour of others for whom they did nothing. Political economists, who were supposed to understand these things, would render a service if they would state the laws of rent and interest in their true light, as relations between one man and another, instead of obscuring the matter by stating the law of rent as a relation between one piece of land which pays rent and another piece which does not pay rent, and the law of wages as a relation between the normal rate of wages in one trade and the normal rate in another, thereby producing a law which is true, but which obscures the ethical aspect of the case by concealing the immoral relation between the worker and the employer who exploits his labour.

*   *   *

The original rules of the **Fabian Society** *might surprise modern Fabians, but they do show where we can find the roots of Labour's Clause IV.*

Declaration of principles of the Fabian Society, 1896

The Fabian Society consists of socialists.

It therefore aims at the re-organization of Society by the emancipation of land and industrial capital from individual and class ownership, and the vesting of them in the community for the general benefit. In this way only can the natural and acquired advantages of the country be equitably shared by the whole people.

The Society accordingly works for the extinction of private property in land and of the consequent individual appropriation, in the form of rent, of the price paid for permission to use the earth, as well as for the advantages of superior soils and sites.

The Society, further, works for the transfer to the community of the administration of such industrial capital as can conveniently be managed socially. For, owing to the monopoly of the means of production in the past, industrial inventions and the transformation of surplus income into capital have mainly enriched the proprietary class, the worker being now dependent on that class for leave to earn a living.

If these measures be carried out, without compensation (though not without such relief to expropriated individuals as may seem fit to the community), rent and interest will be added to the reward of labour, the idle class now living on the labour of others will necessarily disappear, and practical equality of opportunity will be maintained by the spontaneous action of economic forces with much less interference with personal liberty than the present system entails.

For the attainment of these ends the Fabian Society looks to the spread of socialist opinions, and the social and political changes consequent thereon, including the establishment of equal citizenship for men and women. It seeks to achieve these ends by the general dissemination of knowledge as to the relation between the individual and Society in its economic, ethical, and political aspects.

*   *   *

G.D.H. Cole *'s first book,* The World of Labour, *announced a new star on Labour's horizon, at the beginning of the First World War. Here the doctrines of Guild Socialism found practical exposition* . . .

An end to slavery

What, I want to ask, is the fundamental evil in our modern Society which we should set out to abolish?

There are two possible answers to that question, and I am sure that very many well-meaning people would make the wrong one. They would answer POVERTY, when they ought to answer SLAVERY. Face to face every day with the shameful contrasts of riches and destitution, high dividends and low wages, and painfully conscious of the futility of trying to adjust the balance by means of charity, private or public, they would answer unhesitatingly that they stand for the ABOLI-TION OF POVERTY.

Well and good! On that issue every Socialist is with them. But their answer to my question is nonetheless wrong.

Poverty is the symptom: slavery the disease. The extremes of riches and destitution follow inevitably upon the extremes of licence and bondage. The many are not enslaved because they are poor, they are poor because they are enslaved. Yet Socialists have all too often fixed their eyes upon the material misery of the poor without realising that it rests upon the spiritual degradation of the slave.

*   *   *

Bertrand Russell's *best-selling little book,* Roads to Freedom, *was written as a 'pot boiler'. Generations of socialists have since enjoyed this work, which retains a vivid relevance.*

Root and branch reform

I do not think any reasonable person can doubt that the evils of power in the present system are vastly greater than is necessary, nor that they might be immeasurably diminished by a suitable form of Socialism. A few fortunate people, it is true, are now enabled to live freely on rent or interest, and they could hardly have more liberty under another system. But the great bulk, not only of the very poor, but of all sections of wage-earners and even of the professional classes, are the slaves of the need for getting money. Almost all are compelled to work so hard that they have little leisure for enjoyment or for pursuits outside their regular occupation. Those who are able to retire in later middle age are bored, because they have not learnt how to fill their time when they are at liberty, and such interests as they once had apart from work have dried up. Yet these are the exceptionally fortunate: the majority have to work hard till old age, with the fear of destitution always before them, the richer ones dreading that they will be unable to give their children the education or the medical care that they consider desirable, the poorer ones often not far removed from starvation. And almost all who work have no voice in the direction of their work; throughout the hours of labour they are mere machines carrying out the will of a master. Work is usually done under disagreeable conditions, involving pain and physical hardship. They only motive to work is wages: the very idea that work might be a joy, like the work of the artist, is usually scouted as utterly Utopian.

But by far the greater part of these evils are wholly unnecessary. If the civilised portion of mankind could be induced to desire their own happiness more than another's pain, if they could be induced to work constructively for improvements which they would share with all the world rather than destructively to prevent other classes or nations from stealing a march on them, the whole system by which the world's work is done might be reformed root and branch within a generation.

*   *   *

Raymond Williams *initiated a gathering of British socialists who helped to produce the May Day Manifesto in 1968. They were disconcerted by the drift of the first Wilson Government, and particularly by the horrors of the Vietnam War. But the disease of poverty and deprivation was already infecting parts of Britain . . .*

May Day manifesto

The need to gain control over the productive process and over real wealth is the same need as that for the extended care of people, in work, education and housing, or in old age, sickness and disability. It is the assertion of different priorities, against the internal and limited priorities of capitalism. Only when there is democratic control, over the whole process of production and investment, can a human distribution be steadily achieved.

This is then the first policy we have learned: that actual human needs, in our real social conditions, cannot be set against the needs of production, as a marginal or residual claim. The continual frustration of these needs, by what are called the realities of debt or modernization, is in fact, as we have shown, the political acceptance of the internal priorities of profit in modern productive conditions.

CHAPTER TEN

Socialism in our Time

John Hughes

*Rather unusually, a debate about socialist objectives has
opened up in Britain; 'rather unusually' since the last serious
discussion developed during and after the 1914-1918 war.
The debate is supposed to take the form of a re-working of the
socialist objectives expressed in the Labour Party's constitution
(many British trade unions have similar objectives written
into their constitutions). It would be a pity if this new
discussion were taken too narrowly or parochially as if it
were merely an affair of the British. The chapter that follows
seeks to address the issues of socialist policy and practice
arising in modern mixed economies, not least European ones,
though it refers frequently to British experience and forms of
organisation. The author's hope is that it can stimulate a
wider discussion that may draw on socialist experience from
elsewhere.*

Points of Departure

The focus of this chapter is not on socialism as some future
and very different kind of economic system. It attempts
instead to view the principles and practice already apparent
as socialists — and many others — have organised and argued
against the many different kinds of damage that commercial
capitalism can do to people and their societies. To speak of
'mixed' economies obviously implies that while capitalist
institutions and market (profit) driven production and
distribution may have a dominant role in economic life, the
whole socio-economic system may be modified by and
contain substantial elements of socialist values, forms of
organisation, and outcomes. This might be seen as involving
a series of 'frontiers of control', capable — under varying

political and economic pressures — of shifting either towards more socialist systems or in the direction of what one might call unrepentant capitalism. ('Thatcherism' can be seen as an example of a substantial and many-sided shift of the 'frontier of control' within the UK's mixed economy.) Changes in forms of ownership are an important dimension of such changes, but there are many other elements of socialist concern to be reviewed. Combining a number of aspects of socialist socio-economic principle and practice could be strategically important in considering what is involved in any transition to a more socialised mixed economy.

Much of the 'ethic' involved in socialist criticism of capitalist organisation emerges from social experience of capitalist practice. Thus the persistent drive of capitalist enterprise and markets to extreme inequality in power and wealth contrasts with egalitarian and democratic citizenship concerns. The development path has involved hectic accumulation and crises, concentration of activity in particular centres and spiralling decline elsewhere (what Myrdal called 'cumulative causation'). Innovation has gone hand in hand with monopoly power, and generated the destruction and displacement of earlier products and processes. The development of workers, communities, the environment has been distorted and damaged both in development and in decline. Notably, people as workers, with their human capital of skill endowment, have been treated as 'costs', alienated through the 'wage-system' (cf. Guild Socialist criticism*), subjected to a 'command' economy of coercive discipline. A persistent feature of socialist criticism has been that the capitalist firm, its property 'rights' and its motivations, neglect, disrupt and distort the social nature of the processes involved and their wider effects. In the 20th Century much of the so-called 'wealth creating' development has hinged on the robber economy of extracting and not replacing the finite resources of the globe with no regard for sustainable development. The struggle for 'profitable' results may lead to overlapping and

---

*See G.D.H. Cole, *Self Government in Industry*, pp.154-155, 'wages paid only when it is profitable to the capitalist to employ labour' . . . 'the wage-worker surrenders all control over the organisation of production' and 'all claim upon the product of labour'.

waste alongside a failure to provide for all; the provision of infrastructure services (utilities, etc.) being an important example. Increasingly the system has been characterised not by competition as conventionally conceived but by the oscillations between competition, collaboration, and takeover of a limited number (hence 'oligopoly') of giant transnational firms; the issues of power and responsibility become socially inescapable.

Socialist criteria?

A one-dimensional socialist agenda might seek to transfer, e.g. to state ownership, the property rights that have enjoyed such license. It is indeed important to identify where such property transfers have in the past (as in the UK) or may in the future meet specific economic and social needs. But the delineation of capitalist development sketched above involves a much wider range of issues of value and practice that have to be brought into focus. Concentration of economic power without social accountability raises a series of issues of social accountability and economic regulation which connect with social democratic political values. (They also pose the question of whether power is concentrated to be diffused later, or transformed in other ways.) The alienating and dictatorial 'wage-system' needs in response more than an adversarial trade union system, and raises questions of social rights and industrial democracy including gender and other forms of discrimination. Growing inequality of wealth, income, and access to resources forces a response which argues from fairness and equality against exclusion. Capitalism's failure to harness resources to meet universal social needs and socially necessary provision for participation in the citizenship of civil society is confronted head on with the direct provision of massive services, and on a widening range, built round both the needs of all and the needs of each. (And this embraces the principle by which Marx distinguished the 'higher' stage of socialism.) Damage to communities and the environment from the limited perspective of profit-centred accounting has to be challenged and prevented in terms of enforced recognition of wider social interests. The agenda could be extended. The point is that these are not haphazard positions to adopt in face of the real nature of unrestrained capitalism; they express a coherent and cumulative sense of shared social needs and concerns. The combined force of these concerns may move towards transcending rather than modifying capitalist organisation, values and relationships. But they are clearly about changing the terms of reference within which society determines the functions of productive capital, and the responsibilities as well as the opportunities accruing to property in various forms of 'ownership'.

About social responsibility

'Business is not responsible for something it causes, and politics is responsible for something over which it has no control'. (Ulrich Beck, *The Risk Society*)

It is crucial for the well-being of society that there should be a developing framework of economic and social responsibilities that have to be accepted and operated by economic enterprises. The responsibilities are likely to be more far-reaching so far as large enterprises are concerned since questions of monopoly power, standard setting, and influence on innovation, are more directly involved.

This assertion of social responsibility should not be seen as 'interference' with rational economic allocation and efficiency but rather the necessary condition for fully rational choice. The wider social costs and benefits involved in enterprise production and distribution need to be brought within the enterprise's accounts and development decisions (the partial accountancy that only looks at costs directly encountered within the firm and only at its revenues will otherwise send the wrong signals). Insofar as such social costs/benefits are quantified and brought into business accounts and reports (e.g. through taxes or levies, through subsidies or rebates) then we can think of the accountancy or audit involved as more fully socialised. Wider access to and debate of such social auditing is an important contribution to social learning. The factors involved in such social costs/ benefits include such matters as environmental concerns, and the development of the human resources involved.

But there will be issues of social values and needs that are not readily quantifiable, or which are so clearly undesirable (as with aspects of pollution, or neglect of safety) as to be prohibited or subject to other forms of direct 'control', such as regulatory agencies. Examples would be misuse of market power (control of monopoly power and behaviour; consumer protection; discriminatory practices). Positive expression of social values may take the form of legislative/regulatory requirements to recognise employee or consumer rights, individual and collective, or provision for employee benefits and their responsible management (occupational pensions as an example).

Development of such frameworks of social responsibility could in their turn be socially divisive if they operated through inadequately accountable state agencies or through elaborate (and slow and expensive) legal processes. This suggests that socialist criteria would emphasize participatory democracy and openness in developing, operating, and monitoring what is done in the name of the social responsibilities of business. Accountability is a key concept; within the economic organisation to shareholders, and employees; externally, to the relevant communities.

It is worth emphasizing that such regulatory agendas are far from being the exclusive concern of 'sovereign' states. Since the power centres of capitalist business are trans-national, the effective recognition — and implementation — of social responsibilities calls for regulatory principles, agencies, and legislative practice involving the extensive sharing of state sovereignty, as with the European Union (with the slow development of regulations carrying through the Social Charter) and international agencies. Within the nation state (or ex-imperial state) local and regional democratic government can link communities that people recognise as their own with both regulatory protection and participation in the necessities of the development process and employment creation.

'According to their needs'
Over a very large and socially critical segment of social and economic organisation in the United Kingdom the control and

deployment of resources and, crucially, the handling of services to users, are not subject to the values and norms of the market economy. Instead of the inequality and exclusion of 'ability to pay', these services are in substantial part (for Thatcherite market norms are being superimposed in a variety of ways, so one cannot say 'wholly') driven by the requirement for a universal and equally accessible provision related to the satisfaction of individual and social need. The range of public services provided in this way is not a static one — indeed, in all logic, it should develop and change as a dynamic economy and open debate in society produce a re-formulation of needs and how needs can best be met.

From the point of view of socialist principle and practice this range of public services is of enormous importance;

(a) They exemplify and develop in practice an ethos of public service and respect for the rights and needs of all citizens. It would seem inevitable that no arbitrary limit can be placed on the sheer potential involved (e.g. in education to secure 'the full and free development of all'), although traditional 'professional' attitudes may seek to harness and control the values and aspirations attached to particular services.

(b) They offer a process of social learning, and expectation, about equality, citizenship, and respect for a variety of needs and concerns in democratic society. They, therefore, set up, on a large scale and in ways that impinge on all, value systems and experience that challenge the norms of commercialism.

(c) They raise inescapably the issue of the social discipline involved in accepting the transfer payments required (from taxation, much of which may fall on 'market' derived income and wealth) to enable social needs to be met more fully instead of being rationed. Finance plays a major role; the scope for re-distribution away from the extreme inequalities engendered by the market is relevant here, but there are real issues of social choice to be faced through the democratic process. At least in *appearance* it may seem as if provision of such services is at the expense of individual purchasing power in the market place (in reality cutting back public services means the economy lurches towards more inequality, deprivation and, not least, unemployment).

In this context it is worth reflecting briefly on the approach adopted in the UK by successive Conservative governments since 1979. A persistent effort has been made to denigrate public spending and especially welfare spending, with pejorative attacks on 'bureaucracy', 'scroungers', 'waste' etc. Elements of local democratic political influence/control (e.g. on education) have been removed or reduced. Public service management/administration structures have been purged, with business replacements and heavy use of the (party) patronage system. Quasi-market systems of 'contracts' and criteria for resource use have been developed; this has been linked with break-up of previous structures into smaller groups encouraged to pursue revenue goals and restricted to pursuit of their own group interest (hospital 'trusts', etc.). Above all, systematic spending constraints have limited resources in face of rising demand and need; this has consciously aimed at accelerating the growth of private sectors of provision. The latter can pursue market growth — from those with ability to pay, of course, not from needs-based priorities — more successfully in face of stagnant or declining standards in the resource-constrained public services, waiting lists, etc. We are used to this phenomenon in health and education, but it also appears in leisure services, and most disturbingly and on a very large and increasing scale in private security services. Here we can identify the complex values, policies, and manipulation of power over resources and their control, involved in shifting the 'frontier of control' within the mixed economy. It may be easier to grasp the nature and *cumulative* significance of socialist values, practice, and future objectives, by a study of its opposite at work in the most fully socialist and socialised segment of the economy.

The public services and the development of future policy towards them has exceptional significance in the modern economy. The stresses and deprivation of an increasingly unequal society put additional strains on services such as health and security; more fundamental programmes for reinforcing preventive measures on illness, accidents, crime, etc. are not as yet in place. Confusion on organisation, value systems, public accountability has to be tackled (as, too, in education). Given the information technology revolution, a greatly strengthened public system of education accessible through life, linked with a coherent communication system using the most advanced technology has become a central requirement for future social and economic development. The choice between a democratised, social-needs based, approach to those questions and the piecemeal, exploitative, approach of capitalist enterprise is of massive importance. But the more locally (regionally) controlled environmental services are also of great social importance as paid work occupies less of adult life. Shared community resources, and environmental access, for creativity and participation as well as for recreation, are determinants of the quality of life. For this and other reasons public transport has to be reinforced, be designed to minimise pollution and congestion, and pushed towards the criteria of the social needs/socialised public service sector (with universal access) and away from the distortions, and ever higher social costs of unregulated private transport.

Common ownership

This section limits itself to a somewhat schematic review of a variety of forms of common ownership, and to brief comment on some aspects of UK experience in relation to that.

A serious discussion is needed as to the evaluation of past experience and possible directions for future organisation of more socialised and socially responsible forms of ownership, management, and objectives. Experimentation and monitoring should be seen as a natural part of the evolution of common ownership; that has not necessarily been evident in the past.

Because of the particular role played by *nationalised industries* in the post-war UK economy, it may be worth prefacing this section by a somewhat terse account of some of the key elements in that experience. The form of the 'public corporation' with its conventional reliance on management expertise which emerged was the one advocated by Herbert Morrison, even though debates and argument inside the Labour movement were led by advocates of a strong element of workers' representation and control. It was ironic that the re-organisation of West Germany's heavy industries immediately after the war offered a more direct and influential role for workers' elected representatives in managerial direction, a sharing of responsibilities, and that this was put through in co-operation with the then British Control Commission at a time when the much stronger UK trade unions were being told they were not yet 'ready' for such a role, and were offered no more than consultation rights of a formal kind.

In a number of cases, public corporations (and the health service) in fact took over local government plants and property which has been built up over many years of 'municipal socialism'; it was not all (fully compensated) transfer from the private sector. A major pressure for such centralised re-organisation was a recognition (in some cases as a result of influential studies and reports) of the need for a planned co-ordination and renovation of an entire 'utility' sector, in place of inadequate and piecemeal earlier development (cf. electricity). The key industry that most needed this was the one that 'got away', steel. Had the early post-war nationalisation been maintained (instead of being largely unwound by the incoming Conservative administration) a re-organisation on the basis of modern integrated steel plants would have gone through in the 1950s, as it actually did in South Wales. Instead the dynastic structure of steel company ownership delayed major reorganisation (under a second attempt at public ownership) until late into the 1960s — disastrously too late.

In general the chosen role for the public corporations meant a heavy use of (borrowed) capital for investment that massively reduced employment in the industries that had earlier been highly labour intensive (coal, railways, steel, the utilities). There was no coherent debate about the fact that the publicly owned sector of productive industry shed employment on a large scale and over a protracted period; little attempt was made to re-think functions, or accept in practice responsibility for job creation; diversification was for much of the time politically blocked (even the 1945 Labour Government had built in guarantees to private industry against diversification — denounced as 'creeping' socialism — in its legislation carrying through public ownership).

Over much of the period the policies actually pursued

meant that the nationalised industries were exploited by capitalist industry; supply contracts for capital equipment, etc., were monopolised by UK firms (often technically backward and cartelised); one purchasing director kept a statuette of a milch-cow on his desk as an ironic comment. Increasingly, the handling of prices, finance, borrowing terms, capital expenditure came under Treasury control, and were used within short-run concerns about inflation, demand management, etc. The routinisation of much of the function of these industries (since innovation, joint-ventures, and so on were substantially repressed) did not help managerial creativity; internal structures had been modelled on the large private sector monopolistic firms, with multi-level hierarchies. Not only was much of this modelled on ICI; there was a moment in the 1950s when the then head of ICI was called in to review Coal Board management and recommended yet another tier of management to add to the four that already existed.

A rethinking of function to extend actual services or development activities to meet social needs was all too limited. Some aspects of this were sustained in railways and their finance (but within a starved investment programme). A good example was the earlier post-war emphasis on rural electrification.

Formal structures of accountability contrasted with the blurred relations of power and intervention between government ministers and departments (and, of course, the Treasury) and the public corporation; government did not take kindly to open accountability and public scrutiny. When an effective House of Commons committee emerged for a while it was subsequently emasculated. (The present writer had the experience in the late 1970s of carrying through independent investigations into a number of nationalised industries backed by the legislated investigatory powers of the Price Commission; it was illuminating for the investigators, but highly unusual for the corporations.)

All this suggests that there is substantially more to the objective of socialising industries and services than the formal process of transfer of ownership. Nor should we neglect the opportunities for effective employee participation, for public accountability, and for careful discussion of social and economic objectives. The organisational forms adopted may also need to be subject to revision and experimentation; the centralised control of massive re-organisation might perhaps have been followed by more diversity and de-centralisation (e.g. perhaps electricity and gas should have been directly linked, within a Scottish region). There could have been more commitment to the idea that a continuing effort was needed to honour the objective of 'the best obtainable system of popular administration and control'.

Different forms

As to the forms that common ownership may take:

i) *Direct governmental administration.* This may mean local government, regional government (when it exists), and national government. In particular, there may be a need for 'hybrids' (e.g. consortia of local authorities), though here some form of subsidiary organisation may operate. Consortia (e.g. of local authorities) for the development of economic and social services are not necessarily limited to adjacent authorities. For example, 'like-minded' local authorities in different regions (or countries) can work together on provision of specialist functions (such as, design, purchasing of supplies, sharing of professional and technical resources, leisure and transport, comparative social research, etc.).

This has been important in education, housing, and land at local government level. Handling of police services has involved an element of shared control. At national government level, the health service has operated through directly appointed boards, but without the degree of separation of public corporations. Defence has also operated as a central government function, not surprisingly. The post office operated as a central government department for most of its existence, and was only given the public corporation form in the UK in the late 1960s.

ii) *Public corporations.* These are still a significant type. They may be particularly useful in managing integrated basic economic activities of an infra-structure kind (such as rail, postal, utility grids). In the UK there is a Housing Corporation with a range of social housing functions; this may represent

a device of the present government to distance local
authorities from such active development of the housing
stock; a consortium of local authorities on a regional or
sub-regional basis might be more directly democratic in
accountability and more connected with the specifics of local
community needs. (In the utility field, co-ordination of
regional energy plcs — instead of separation into gas/
electricity/etc. — might be more useful than the previous
corporation structure, or than the present regulatory regime
in Britain.)

iii) *'Social ownership'* such as Trusts (cf. National Trust);
this is a form that could be encouraged and widely developed.
The flexible development of 'social' housing might use such
a form. Where there are a variety of social views and opinions,
'Trusts' that are not profit orientated may be socially
preferable to the kind of commercial concentrations of power
that have emerged in the media.

iv) *Co-operatives and Mutual Societies.* Co-operatives may
have been in retreat in the retail trade sector, in face of the
vast economies of scale of the multiples, but they constitute
a varied and experienced range of activities, e.g. in
agricultural supply and purchasing. A fresh look at the
potential for employment creation and viable development
through the co-operative form is called for. Mutual societies,
such as building societies and credit unions have great further
potential in handling a variety of finance and credit needs of
ordinary households and groups of employees or local people
with a common bond of interest. Here, too, there should be
thought as to how to stimulate their internal democracy,
provide them with more support services, and identify new
patterns of shared objective that can make use of their form
of shared ownership and control. (Recent moves to bribe
existing members in building societies to sell-out their stake
and effectively hand over to conventional joint-stock limited
companies should be resisted.)

v) *Workers' capital funds — especially pension funds.* The
particular significance of the pension funds is that they
manage, as trustees for the fund, members' funds that are
deferred pay transformed into capital. In the UK their scale
and the deployment of their assets is of enormous significance

— but their *potential* role is far greater. In recent years their total assets have reached a market value of around £500 billion (that is, £500,000 million); most significantly over half of these take the form of equity share holdings in UK companies. It has been estimated that this combined share ownership of the UK pension funds represents around one-third of all UK company equity capital. (Other 'institutional' shareowners, notably insurance companies, account for another third of the total.) Since the mid-1970s the share of total UK equity capital held by the pension funds has doubled, while that held by 'persons' has halved. The pension funds have around eleven million worker contributors and millions of retired-worker recipients. Collectively these workers ('by hand and brain') are the most massive and rapidly growing force in 'ownership' in UK industry, commerce, and finance.

The social potential of that 'ownership' has not yet been realised. Even democratic control and membership accountability within the funds is inadequate. Within the right legislative framework these funds could operate with democratic and socially responsible guidelines, and with the full participation of the employees collectively involved — working and retired. The 'trustee' role, and the social accountability that needs to go with it, is highly important. These organisations break down through shared ownership of capital the great divide between labour and capital in industrial society. The active and socially responsible use by such funds of their massive combined stakes in equity holdings could change the social role of shareholders and shareholding (e.g. in forcing the pace of better 'governance' of joint-stock companies).

The historic irony is that these funds grew out of the self-interest of the senior administrative and managerial — including directorial — personnel of big companies; they did not want the worst features of the wage-system to apply to themselves, so asset-backed 'funded' pension schemes were developed for them, helped by a privileged tax position for such funds. The base of participation widened over time, and with growing trade union understanding of what was at stake.

It may seem an unusual starting point for a breakthrough from the old wage-system towards a more socialised recognition of employee rights and income needs, and for a transformation of previously polarised property relationships. For many part-time women workers discrimination still leaves them outside this particular transcendance or did, but now the social responsibilities and employee rights enforced through new European institutions are coming to their rescue.

vi) *Joint-stock companies*. Public ownership has on many occasions used the joint stock company form (possibly operating under a state holding company). This was important in the 1960s/1970s when a number of important UK firms were faced with bankruptcy and extinction, and had this been accepted would have resulted in major damage to the economy through loss of exports, collapse of employment, and so on. The 'rescue' of such enterprises as Rolls Royce and British Leyland created an opportunity for re-organisation under state ownership on a more advanced and efficient basis; this could be seen as continuing on a long-term basis, or involving subsequent sale as a commercial company (i.e. a changing portfolio of publicly owned companies going through a rehabilitation process).

More widely, the joint-stock form does represent to a limited extent a form of social organisation of capital; developments in company legislation, social regulation, and new patterns of shareholding activity, could move this form of property organisation towards a more social and participatory use and control of capital, bringing employees, shareholders, and local communities into more active representation and constructive roles.

It is already possible to see a growing sense of the importance of an *active* use of 'institutional' (especially pension fund) shareholder influence on company policy and 'governance'. Certainly the old passivity of these large scale 'institutional' equity holdings was socially indefensible and left so-called 'private ownership' as an empty box category in an economic system steered by largely non-accountable top executives of giant firms. So we should greet the British TUCs recent issue of 'Guidelines' on shareholder voting to the member trustees on the boards of pension funds as a welcome straw in the wind. Consciously designed to strengthen the current emphasis on active fund intervention through combined shareholding pressure on companies, the 'Guidelines' were drafted for the TUC by PIRC (Pensions Investment Research Consultants) which has for some time been working with 'like-minded' pension funds of progressive local authorities to develop a new force for socially responsible company behaviour.

But if the participatory rights and power of shareholders as 'stakeholders' in the joint stock company are to be emphasised and made effective — thus giving real social function to social ownership — so too should we emphasise the rights and representation of other stakeholders concerned with company development — notably the employees. Pension fund trustees exercising share-owning rights (and social responsibilities) on behalf of their members (workers by hand and brain) should be complemented by representative employee (workers by hand and brain) in an evolving process of shared participation, co-determination, within the organised form of the joint-stock company. Reform of company law for such purposes should be seen as part of a socialist agenda to strengthen the rights — and responsibilities of social ownership.

Conclusion

Having announced a debate, Labour's Leader appears genuinely hurt if anyone else seeks to speak in it. When 32 Labour MEPS endorsed the statement which is featured at the beginning of this book, this raised eyebrows, and they were asked not to debate the matter until Tony Blair had visited Brussels. When some of those involved advertised their view, they were rather sharply reprimanded. This article was written and offered in turn to Tribune, The New Statesman, *and* The Guardian. *All were unable to find space for it, and in the case of the weeklies this was a genuine reason. So it was given to* The Daily Telegraph. *Miraculously, space at once appeared in* The Guardian *the very next day, to traduce its author.*

How to conduct a debate?

Labour's new Leader, Tony Blair, came out to Brussels to meet with the European Parliamentary Labour Party. One of the reasons for his visit was that he wished to explain his views about the revision of the Labour Party's constitution. At the same time, he clarified Labour's attitudes to European Union, and delivered a speech to a dinner attended by prominent business people, aimed to raise funds for the Labour Party.

A majority of members of the EPLP are opposed to the Leader's attempts to change Labour's constitution. They were opposed before he came, and they are still opposed. Most of them are quite happy to have a discussion, aimed at agreeing a medium-term programme, and concerned to elaborate on the Party's values. But they do not approve of an attempt to eliminate the socialist part of Labour's constitution. Thirty-two Members signed a statement along these lines, in the Autumn of 1994. Various advertisements were taken in socialist newspapers to explain this view.

On the day before the Blair visit another advertisement was placed in *The Guardian*, shortly before the Labour Leader set off to Brussels. It provoked a storm of controversy, although in fact it added nothing to what had been said two months and more earlier. Various people complained about the advertisement on the grounds that it might have detracted from the reception of the Leader's message to the business community. Having carefully examined the newspapers, I can see no evidence of any such effect.

It might be thought somewhat ingenuous to invite a debate and then complain when people respond. However, a deal of moral energy was wasted on this entirely peripheral issue, so that the much vaunted exchange on Clause IV itself was greatly restricted.

The new Leader gave a short introduction, adding nothing to what had already been said about his reasons for seeking constitutional change. He has a very pleasant manner, although on this occasion his winning smile looked a little strained, even nervous. But he came across as an open, bright, young man, with a simple faith in the evident commonsense of his viewpoint.

However, even before he spoke, there was some evidence of the managerial quality of his minders, who had been kind enough to announce from Labour Party headquarters that nobody cared what MEPs said, because they were all "nonentities". Of course, such gratuitous insults would not help in the understanding of the issues involved in this discussion, if it really were a discussion.

Mr Blair told us that he thought that all the European Socialist Parties had modified their constitutions. However, his researchers had briefed him rather badly on this question, and he was clearly unaware of the profound anti-capitalist sentiments expressed in the constitution of the French Socialist Party, and of any of the ideas of the Swedish socialists on common ownership through Employee Investment Funds and collective capital formation.

Unfortunately, there was no time to talk about these things, although I tried to raise some of them. The Leader gave it as his opinion that nobody believed in wholesale nationalisation, except for supporters of North Korea. North Korean supporters are no more visible in the EPLP than they are in Westminster (possibly even less so), so this argument did not seem very persuasive. But perhaps it contributed to the general view, which we now know to have been assiduously hawked outside, to the newspapers by the minders, that the Leader had "laid down the law", and "shown his strength", by winning a famous victory over a non-existent opponent.

Actually this newspaper hype is quite unfair to the Leader. He was on his best behaviour. The most severe thing that he said was that he thought the famous *Guardian* advertisement to have been discourteous. When he told someone to "grow up" he said it almost whimsically. Only when we read the press accounts did we learn that this was to be understood to constitute the equivalent of a flogging.

The Labour MEPs have come from a very wide range of different backgrounds. It would be difficult to find a grouping more representative of the present day Labour Party. And indeed, the present day Labour Party itself is making it absolutely clear that the MEPs views are almost universally shared by Labour Party members. As the returns come in, it is perfectly plain that Labour members are not at all anxious to make their peace with market capitalism, and do not accept that the pursuit of equality is consonant with unbridled competition. It is very easy to misrepresent the disagreements which thus arise, and to attribute them to some kind of personal animus. But the tantalisingly brief exchange in the EPLP leads me to think that this would be quite wrong.

The short truth is that there is a fundamental political disagreement between socialists: all socialists, any socialists, on the one side, and the Leader of the Labour Party on the other. He is, quite simply, a Liberal. He is sufficiently open and pleasant to give the impression that it would be quite easy to work with him on a variety of civil problems, although he would not be very radical about most of them. But the frustration which is rising on the left arises from the fact that this young man has not the faintest idea of how socialists think, and does not begin to understand the mentality of the Party which he has been elected to lead. It is certainly aggravated by the ruthless news management by the star cynics who filter his views across to the media.

This is perhaps the most fascinating puzzle in modern British politics. Maybe it is a sign of a terminal crisis in the Labour Party's evolution. The problem is quite stark. Global capitalism is more powerful than it has ever been, and its power is more concentrated in fewer major centres. It has, to a large extent, destroyed the effective economic powers of small and medium nation states. This is why Socialist Parties find it very difficult to focus their actions for full employment, for instance. The individual states of Europe are not strong enough to determine effective alternative macro-economic policies. It might have been possible to try to come to grips with this enormous difficulty. But Tony Blair's solution has been to imagine that the problem does not exist.

Nowhere in the drafts which have been circulated through the Labour Party does the word "capitalism" feature. But the polarisation of modern societies flows directly from the concentration of economic power. Why have all those privatisations been driven forward? Clearly they have been immensely profitable, and they have also contributed to the further adverse concentration of power. Do the legions of the unemployed not suffer from this process? Is the recurrence of mass poverty nothing to do with it?

Mr Blair offers us pleasant phrases about equality and social justice. But he will put no robber barons in the dock. Indeed, he explained with great candour why he could make no consequent policy on anything until after he had been elected.

The conclusion which I drew from all of this was very sad. If the Labour Party can come under this kind of influence, what use will it be to any of our people? Wherever I go in my Constituency, I meet those who have been uprooted from work. I meet people driven to slave for poverty wages, or subsisting on the margins of life on miniscule benefits. I encounter wholesale spoliation of the environment in the exploitation of its resources. Capitalism is with us every day of the week, and its effect is consistently evil. It saps the morale of the poor and excluded population. It drives those who are able to find work to exert themselves for longer and longer hours, and often for smaller and smaller rewards, in order to avoid the ultimate stigma of unemployment. To speak of equality in our sad mining villages is to mock everything that is holy.

Socialism certainly needs to be re-invented. Old-fashioned nationalisation will not be restored, any more than the monasteries, the patrimony of the poor in the middle ages. But common ownership is more and more the necessary response to runaway private acquisitiveness, and the infinite destruction wrought by greed. It will advance through the democratisation of pension funds and similar forms, and through joint and common international action to match and pace the multinationals.

All this is very old hat, and Mr Blair and his bright young acolytes will take great pleasure in pointing out that much of it has been said before.

We must find ways of continuing to say it, if they steal the Labour Party away from us, and return it to the worship of the accomplished power. Perhaps they will not be able to do this. It is difficult to believe that Labour cannot be better than this in 1995.